FOREWORD BY JAN

CW01499058

The chance to make music should b
have only to watch young children responding to music through
song, movement or other activities—to recognise how integral it can
be to their personal, social and intellectual development. Some are
lucky enough to receive this encouragement at home but sadly many
children miss out on opportunities like these in their early years. All
too few of the teachers who work with young children feel sufficiently confident to engage in musical activities with their classes,
and changes in musical education provision over the years have
tended to exacerbate, rather than to improve, this situation. Where
access to music is concerned, inequality of opportunity prevails.

The scheme set out in this book is intended as an individual con-
tribution to help improve this position. Aware of the concerns of
many of those teachers working with the under fives who would
gladly make music with their classes if only they had the support to
enable them to do so, Ting Randle has documented in a clear and accessible way a scheme that she herself has evolved over more than a
decade in her work with early years children. The scheme has developed and been tested out through her contact with teachers and advis-
ers in the various schools and centres in which she has worked. It is
largely at their request, and with their encouragement, that she has
now made it available for others to share.

While simple in its conception and layout, and making no demands for prior musical expertise, the scheme manages to provide a
secure grounding in those basic musical elements from which further
development can occur. An experienced musician and teacher, Ting
Randle is able to blend the knowledge and understanding that she has
gained at first-hand through her career and with members of her own
family. She describes, in language that demonstrates the depth of her
own 'hands on' experience, an easily memorable pattern of activities
around which early musical learning of a fruitful kind can be structured and shows how teachers can make these their own, then vary
and extend them. The book is generous in the provision of materials
that can be photocopied and used, and in the lists of available books,
recordings and other resources that teachers are likely to find helpful
when working with early years children. The ideas here offer natural
links to national curriculum requirements.

For those who are keen to find a way to get started, and who are
looking for a helpful and supportive guide, I commend this account

7

of The Triangle Club Music Scheme to you. Try it for yourself, and there is every chance that music can come alive in your class, your school. And, once you have begun, the children themselves will help you take things forward.

Janet Ritterman
London, April 2004

www.ting-randle.co.uk

TRIANGLE CLUB

A Music Scheme for the
Under Fives

by

TING RANDLE

with a foreword by
DAME JANET RITTERMAN
**Director of the Royal College of Music
London**

photographs by
CATHERINE HUDSON

and graphic illustrations by
PETE RANDLE

THE TRIANGLE CLUB MUSIC SCHEME HANDBOOK

First published 2004

ISBN 1-904408-02-8

Published by BANK HOUSE BOOKS
www.bankhousebooks.com

Printed and bound by Lightning Source.

Layout, repro and typesetting by

BANK HOUSE BOOKS
PO Box 3
NEW ROMNEY
TN29 9WJ

Photography: CATHERINE HUDSON
Graphics and illustrations: PETE RANDLE

This book is dedicated to
Rupert, Lily, Kitty and Bertie

Author's Note

I have been thinking about this book intermittently over the past year. Ideas about it change. Ideas about who are to be the potential users of the book, about the children to whom it is to be taught, about the way it will be interpreted. Without assuming too much importance for such a small book, I can see the immense value of the learning within it if it can be used creatively.

I have been into several schools with the scheme now to show teachers and children alike the magical place that is the world of music, and each of these schools has taught me so much about the scheme and its value.

The emphasis in some of the schools has been on a very organised, structured use of my scheme, with the children disciplined to sit and listen to me as they are encouraged to sit and listen to others throughout their school day. Even the movement activities are rigorously structured. In one school markers were placed on the floor to inform the children which way they should move around the room.

The interesting thing is the amount of learning that takes place even when the children seem to be inattentive.

Dipping in and out of learning is something we do as adults all our lives. With the government's initiatives for Life Long and Family Learning, this learning we all do throughout life is being acknowledged and encouraged and highly-valued. We begin learning like this as young children. We are drawn to things, bright colours, noises, tastes, things that move, and our attention is held and an impression made that does not go away, but remains, to become part of an inheritance that moulds us into who we are. There is an element of magic surely to what we learn and how we learn it! I believe this, but I believe equally strongly that all children and all adults do not have equal access to this magic and the process of acquiring it.

If my book can open a window, giving learners of all ages access to something they otherwise would not have access to, then it has done its work, for an open window is all that is needed to gain a glimpse of another world.

The implication throughout has been that an holistic approach to teaching is the most positive approach to developing a curriculum for those critically important Early Years. I wish also to reiterate here that, although this book uses music and ideas which are specifically Western in orientation, I am fully aware of the fact that 'holism is a

multi-cultural concept; a relatively recent discovery in the West, holistic philosophies have long been prominent in Indian, Chinese and African civilisations (eg the Indian festival of Holi, the Chinese spiritual philosophy of Tao).' [Hazaeesingh, Simms & Anderson, p80, 1989]. This is to encourage the users of this book to understand that the eight activities included here are such that the finer details of what is chosen to be taught, and the songs to be sung, can be as varied as there is music in this world to be heard and instruments to play it on. My own education has been shaped by certain experiences which have led me along a certain path in my choice and taste. This is mine and it need not be yours. I have given you a guide to what has proved successful for me and with the children (and adults) I've taught.

This guide is simply the first step of what will be a life long journey of discovery and learning which will develop the whole child. There needs to be this positive approach to learning that is for life. There also needs to be an awakening of the child's emotional, spiritual, social and cognitive qualities which will allow him or her to develop into an adult who feels he/she belongs emotionally, spiritually and socially to the community in which he/she is living. A positive Early Years curriculum will sow the seed which will begin this development.

Ting Randle
August 2nd 2003

The education of early childhood
should be based entirely upon this principle:
assist the natural development of the child.

Maria Montessori[1]

Preface

I feel there is an urgent need for music to be made available to all children. I believe that the younger you can begin with them, the better. I devised **The Triangle Club Music Scheme** as a structured scheme of carefully chosen activities to teach music to groups of children aged three and four. It has met with great enthusiasm and success since I began teaching it twelve years ago.

Recently I was asked to deliver my scheme to a group of childcare providers. It was the first time I had done such a thing. I set out my aims and objectives and showed how these can be met. I also showed the playgroup leaders how the scheme links directly into other areas of the curriculum for the under fives. The benefits to children go beyond that of simply developing musical awareness, making it a real and valuable adjunct to lesson plans. At the end of the hour I was asked, "Could we buy your book?" And I had to say that there was not one.

I then saw that for the scheme to be able to reach a large number of children, and for it to be an ongoing concern, I needed to be able to share it. I began to think seriously about the benefit of having a book that could be used in pre-school, or indeed by any groups where there are a number of young children. Parents and grandparents might like to use it too.

This book is the result, complete with my scheme.

The Triangle Club Music Scheme is the answer for all those playgroup leaders and childcare providers who realise the importance of early music training for young children, but do not quite know how to go about teaching music, or what to teach. All you need to teach this scheme are enthusiasm and the ability to follow a scheme of work.

My intention is to provide all those involved with pre-school children with the means to give those children a comprehensive early musical education. One that is interesting, exciting and informative for your children, and one that is easy for you to follow, and enables you to feel confident

about teaching. To this end, I have been at pains always to keep in mind what it is that children need to know, whilst at the same time making the scheme a viable concern for you, the childcare providers. I am aware that some of you may be learning alongside your children, and for this reason, I have made the scheme clear and accessible for those of you who have little musical knowledge yourselves.

You can see from the way the material has been set out that if you choose to, you can initially ignore a substantial amount of the book, whilst still giving your children a wonderful introduction to music. As you grow in confidence, you may find that you want to delve more deeply into it.

The scheme offers value, great fun and immense enjoyment.

Ting Randle
Wells, February 2003

Contents

Introduction

Music is important. Acquiring knowledge of it develops many skills. It alleviates many pressures in this life. It is all around us, and continues to inspire us. Even those who confess to knowing nothing about music are deeply affected by it, can express an opinion about it, and will be happy to offer a value judgement about it. It speaks to each one of us, and appeals to a place inside us that has variously been linked to the emotional, the physical, the spiritual, and the intellectual. It has had many claims made for it. For example, Don Campbell's book **The Mozart Effect** has recently linked music with health, well-being, and greater intelligence.[2]

The Neglect of Music Education

I have been interested in music education for many years, both in the place it holds outside mainstream education, and in the place it holds in general education inside educational establishments. As a class music teacher, I have often been frustrated by the brief time allotted to music lessons, and by the demands of the curriculum. As an instrumental teacher, I have often been frustrated by lack of time in which to teach music to my pupils, to teach what needs to be learned to facilitate the making of a 'musician', alongside teaching them the skill needed to play the piano. I am only too aware of the lack of preparation and dearth of general knowledge about music that most children have when they come for their first instrumental lesson. In general, much more could be done to educate young children about music, whether or not they choose to learn an instrument.

Music education is important for the development of the whole individual, for not just emotional development, but also physical, spiritual and intellectual.

It is generally acknowledged that the awakening of an aesthetic understanding is important in the development of the

whole child. However, the argument for logical reasoning and intellectual science always seems to come first in the building of a curriculum for children. If, as is often suggested, a child learns to organise his experience through his aesthetic understanding too, do we not then need to strengthen and develop this aspect of a child's makeup?

But music has a low profile in many schools, even though it is a foundation subject in the National Curriculum for England and Wales and is compulsory in primary schools. The idea of it, however, as an optional activity lingers on in some schools, whether because of the fear of having to teach a specialist subject, or simply the widely-held belief that music is a poor relation to other subjects. Whatever the reason, the government is doing much to address this and there is abundant evidence available to show the tremendous value of music education, and the benefit to all areas of a child's development.

Over the years, music in schools has been asked to fulfil a variety of functions. Views on how and what to teach have become so confused that it has frustrated the ideal. Plato, in his ideas about how the ideal citizen would be educated as far back as c.320 BC, saw music education as something which could stimulate the emotions and nurture sensitivity, but he also believed it to be a powerful force in developing the physical and the intellectual being. Often, only such a diluted account of what should be taught reaches the teacher and child alike that it renders music education almost worthless, and adds weight to the argument that music taught in schools is a waste of time.

Who Should Teach Music?

Who should teach music has often been a cause for concern too, and has been instrumental in adding confusion to the debate about music education. A problem which often seems insurmountable is the lack of confidence most teachers feel when it comes to the teaching of music to children. In my

experience this general feeling of inadequacy applies not only to teachers of pre-school children but also to primary school teachers. Teaching music often gets neglected in the primary school because a teacher feels he or she simply does not have the knowledge or the skill to teach the subject to his or her class.

There has been a good deal of research done into whether the teaching of primary school music should be carried out by a specialist or by the class teacher. It is not my intention within the limitations of this book, where my main concern is with the teaching of pre-school children, to delve too deeply into this. I just want to draw attention to the fact that music education in general throughout pre-school and primary education in many countries is sadly in a distressed state.

Are All Children Musical?

More confusion over the teaching of music arises from terminology.

What does it mean to be a musician or to be musical? Is the definition of being musical having the ability to play an instrument? Being able to compose a piece of music? Being able to listen to and appreciate a piece of music? Any music, or are we referring only to our western definition of 'high art music'? If we can define what we mean by being a musician or being musical, can we then know what it is that needs to be taught in order to become such a thing?

Confusion has already crept in here. Already I have seemingly sought to separate two clearly related terms. Is it not necessary to be musical to be a musician? Yes. But clearly you do not have to be a musician to be musical. Someone who can appreciate music is musical, yet need not be able to play an instrument, in the same way that someone who is literate need not be a writer. *And it is my belief that all children are born with an ability to become musical,* in the same way that all children are born with the ability to become literate. *And if the ability is there it can be awakened, developed and refined.*

When Should Music Be Taught?

I have described some of the many confusions which attach themselves to the idea of music and the teaching of it, and contribute to it still being something of a ridiculed subject in non-specialist schools. What is it that sets music apart from most other subjects, and makes children and teachers and parents alike wary of it? I have given this some thought, and it occurs to me that the problem lies not only in *how* or *what* is best to teach in music, or in *who* should teach music, but in *when* to teach it.

Early in 2001, I went to a seminar given by NAME, The National Association of Music Educators, in which much was spoken of in relation to making music more accessible. One phrase struck me then and continues to come back to me about pre-school music education specifically. One of the lecturers suggested that from pre-school onwards there should be a continuum for music education. Each stage, the speaker propounded, should have equal status, and all levels should attract the best teaching.

Most people would agree that the earlier you begin to learn anything the better. And there is much evidence to support this theory. Teaching a child to play an instrument in order to become an instrumentalist is not always possible or desirable at a very young age, but that is not to say that music cannot be taught. Indeed, much preparation can be carried out early on with young children. Maria Montessori wrote in **The Discovery of the Child**, "The development of the senses actually precedes that of the higher intellectual faculties, and in a child between the ages of three and six it constitutes his formative period. We can therefore assist the development of the senses during this period."[3]

It is in this early teaching of music that I am interested. And not just as an isolated exercise.

Pre-School Music Education

If you can begin teaching music to a child at three and four years, how much more able the child will then be to appreciate music generally, regardless of whether or not he goes on to play an instrument.

If one of a teacher's main aims is to teach children how to discriminate, then an early introduction to music can provide an easy way to enable young children to do this. If it is possible to show a child the difference between a triangle and a jingle stick, or an oboe and a clarinet, surely it is only the next step to provide them with the tools to discriminate. They can be taught to do this firstly in general terms, and then by using a more precise language. They can learn to be able to talk about music, to describe it, and then to use it to communicate.

Communication is a valuable tool for a child. To express oneself one needs a language. If the language is learnt early it becomes an easy means of communication. There is a free and confident use of it to express one's feelings and describe what is important around one. A child learns to feel connected to, and part of, the world in which he lives if he is able to make himself understood. *Music has a language. It can be learnt.*

With the child who does start learning an instrument, there is great delight in awakening him to his discovery of music through learning to play the instrument. But life would be much easier for the instrumental teacher if the child came with a basic understanding and appreciation of music. And, more importantly, life would be much richer for the child.

It would be much easier if the child could sing a simple melodic line; clap a rhythm; feel the difference between a crotchet and a quaver; feel moved by a variety of musical sounds; tell the difference between the sound of an oboe and a clarinet; hear a minor chord and be able to explain to you its character and describe it to you, however simply; be able to tell you how clever Prokofiev was to choose the bassoon to portray the grumpy old grandfather in **Peter and the Wolf,**

"because it can be made to sound gruff and grumpy." And why? "Because of its size." If the child had a musical language already, by which he could communicate, how much easier the instrumental teacher's job would be.

And if you can begin teaching all this to the child in pre-school, he will have a rich vocabulary, and a good, basic knowledge from which he can draw to express himself.

Why then not begin musical education in pre-school? And what is to stop us giving it the best teaching?

The Triangle Club Music Scheme
The Triangle Club Music Scheme, which I devised specifically for three and four year olds, offers the very best strategy for giving children the tools they need to build on in later life.

About the Triangle Club Music Scheme

T he Triangle Club Music Scheme is a tightly structured programme, designed as a year's scheme which is taught to groups of three and four year olds on a weekly basis, throughout term times.

Each weekly session consists of eight carefully selected music and movement activities, which are laid out in this book (Chapter 3). The scheme is closely prescribed, which makes it accessible and easy for anybody to follow. You need have no prior knowledge of music teaching and no prior musical training. My scheme links into other areas of the curriculum, and by doing so, into other areas of a child's development. The course is tried and tested, and has been extremely successful and popular over the twelve years it has been in use.

Aims and Objectives of the Scheme

The main aim of **The Triangle Club Music Scheme** is to give young children the opportunity to develop their musical awareness and their self-confidence in handling the medium of sound. This can be done in a number of ways, through practical experience and creative musicianship. The scheme aims to provide children with an enjoyable and rewarding introduction to music and music-making.

Methods of the Scheme

Discovering the elements of music through games, singing and playing instruments whilst developing the ear enables young children to benefit from early music training in a playful and relaxed manner. This serves as a valuable introduction to music for all children whether or not they continue with more formal instrumental lessons.

Children are taught the basic ingredients of music. As with a cake mixture, there are a few fundamental ingredients which together form the vital mixture of musical sound. Each of

these elements - rhythm, pitch, tempo, dynamics, timbre, for example - forms a starting point for discovering the way that music works. Listening to these sounds creates and helps to develop a basic aesthetic awareness.

Group Work

Children often feel inhibited in some areas, such as singing and composition, when working individually. Working in groups helps to overcome any such feelings. For older children, group compositions can be recorded and written down with the use of simple signs and symbols. (There are photocopiable examples of this 'graphic notation' in Appendix 2, and further examples in Chapter 3.) Children have a great sense of achievement when they see their own manuscripts, however simple, and hear their own compositions. In this way, the connection between sight and sound is encouraged and clarified at an early stage. This development of basic 'reading' skills is crucial.

Listening Skills

The art of listening is in many ways the most important skill a musician needs to acquire. We spend considerable time on listening games, proceeding to learn about the orchestra and the different families of instruments which give us such a rich variety of sound. We listen to many types of music, such as jazz, popular and classical, and to music from a variety of cultures.

Music is a performing art. There is no right or wrong way of being creative, and every child has something valuable to contribute. **The Triangle Club Music Scheme** offers all children the opportunity to develop skills which will inevitably enable them to enjoy music more, to express themselves through sound in the same way they can through words and pictures, and most important of all, to have fun learning about the wonderful world of music.

Learning the Language of Music

Children, like adults, learn in a variety of ways. **The Triangle Club Music Scheme** tries to deal with all the different ways we can learn, relying on imitation, repetition and doing. These are the ways that children learn best in their early stage of development.

Teaching in the early stages is mainly done by good example. Imitation is how we initially learn every skill. Children need a period of time in which they can listen to and absorb this new language. Children are very receptive at three and four years of age.

This music course aims to tap into the child's natural curiosity, to encourage its development and channel its progression into exploring and discovering not only the wonderful world of musical sound, but also into discovering each child's ability.

Confidence is the prerequisite of all learning and, as I said earlier, there is no right or wrong way of being creative, this course should positively encourage all children to grow in confidence as they have fun learning about music.

Some Benefits of the Scheme

In early childhood, play is linked quite strongly to the pleasure a young child feels when he has mastered something. We all know how children like to experience control. Many of the activities in this programme give the child direct contact with this feeling. They learn how to control their voices, their bodies, their thoughts. And they also learn how to control the sound various instruments make, both when they are playing them and, as in the conducting exercise in Activity Six, when others are.

The important thing with very young children is to keep the frustration level down, whilst stimulating them sufficiently to

26

keep their interest. By providing them with a coherent framework from which they can learn, music can be made relevant and available to all pre-school children.

We all know how receptive the young child is, how curious he is, and how delighted he is when he learns how to do something. As we have seen, this scheme enhances confidence. Maria Montessori wrote that, 'If teaching is to be effective with young children, it must assist them to advance on the way to independence."[4] The scheme enables each child to develop an awareness of music through activity, bearing in mind Montessori's comment that, "We never stop to think that a child who does not act does not know how to act."[5]

The programme will awaken and develop a child's sensibilities; his mind; his will; his memory; his concentration; his language skills; his control over bodily movements and thoughts, and control over his sound world specifically, but also his environment generally. All these skills can be developed through the discovery of the wonderful world of music. As educators, it is our job to awaken, develop and refine.

Links with Other Areas of the Curriculum

Each of the eight activities feeds into other areas of the curriculum, developing skills in children which are very important and vital. And herein lies **The Triangle Club Music Scheme**'s great strength. It can be used to reinforce in a fresh and interesting way the many tasks and commitments of early years educators.

The author is well aware of the early learning goals for the foundation stage, and knows that this music scheme links into and consolidates many other areas of the curriculum, to encourage children's development in those other areas. Using the scheme will encourage:

- personal, social and emotional development;
- language and literacy;
- mathematical development;

- knowledge and understanding of the world;
- physical development; and
- creative development.

(The Foundation Stage Curriculum is statutory nationally for children aged three to five years.)

Extension of the Scheme

As you become more and more immersed in the teaching of **The Triangle Club Music Scheme**, several things will happen. You will see the beauty of the scheme in its basic form; you will see its inherent infallibility, but also its limitations. And you will want to develop it yourself. With the aid of the extension activities contained in this book, your knowledge of young children, and your continued use of the scheme, you will be able to develop the programme within the context of your playgroup. In this way, it will never get boring for you. (After all, although it is a year's short course for the children, you will be teaching year after year.)

It takes forty-five minutes to work through each of the eight basic activities which make up a session. The children enjoy each activity. It is suggested that you use all eight activities every week as a whole package. That way, you can be assured the children are learning about all aspects of music. But it is also made clear in Chapter 4 how easy it is to extend each activity. Used in this way, you will find the scheme extremely versatile, and will begin to see how it can be adapted to fit into the curriculum for the under fives. It can also be altered to fit into your own busy timetable and to suit your own pre-school. For example, perhaps you do not have all the children coming on 'music day', so you might want to adapt the scheme, so as to offer parts of it on more than one day and make sure that every child is getting some music tuition every week.

It is hoped that as you read the course activities, you will see how this is possible.

I make no claims here to have discovered any great and

new method. This has been done already by very great musical minds such as Emile Jacques Dalcroze, Carl Orff, Kodaly and many others; really brilliant educators who had great vision and a passion for their subject that went beyond the normal daily chore of teaching and into the realms of magic. This is the extra ingredient with extraordinary minds and it is present in their teaching. I have not created a method. I have picked over, and borrowed from, adapted and revised, and enjoyed every minute of it, to come up with a plan that *works*.

The material I use has all been used before. Where I think the beauty of my scheme lies is in the format. Its conciseness appeals to the pre-school leader for two reasons: it is easily understood and, while it is in some respects prescriptive, it allows scope for development and variation. The scheme can be used as it stands without any further thought from the teacher, and it would still encourage the early development of a child's musical awareness. My scheme shows you *what* to teach and *how* to teach it. And that is all you need to know to get started.

Using the Scheme – The Practicalities

Before moving on to the activities which make up the scheme itself, let us look at some practical aspects of using the programme.

Your Qualifications

No musical training is necessary. All you need to teach this scheme are knowledge and love of teaching pre-school children, enthusiasm, and the ability to follow a scheme of work.

The whole scheme has been described very simply. Supporting material has also been included in the appendices; for example, in Appendix 7, the musical terms used in this book are explained, and in Appendix 6, the different families of instruments are shown.

You may be worried about singing. Adults often say that they have no singing voice, and if you are anxious about it, then simply sing along to a tape in the sessions.

Make sure you know the songs well, as this will give you the confidence you need to proceed with the object of the activity, which is to enjoy singing! The vital thing here, as in all the activities, is that you participate, and lead the children, showing obvious enjoyment. It is important for the children to see you 'doing', as it is this which then in turn gives them the confidence to 'do' too. As with all the activities, your enthusiasm is the essential ingredient in bringing the session to life.

You do not need to be able to read music. You will probably already know many of the songs which are recommended here. If you cannot read music, and are concerned about how you will be able to use songs you do not already know (such as those which have been written specially for the scheme), I suggest that you just get a friend who *can*

read music to sing or play the songs on the piano and record them. You could then learn the tunes from tape. Nor do you need to be able to play the piano or recorder; again, you could use a tape when necessary.

Other Adults

You teach the scheme on your own, without any helpers (although, if you know a pianist, it might be useful for them to come and play for you). Parents do not stay with their children, except occasionally when a child needs a parent there to help them settle in their first week.

Children's Age Range

The scheme is designed for pre school and reception age children.

Group Size

The programme works best in a situation where there are about ten to fifteen children.

Where You Work

You need a room where there is enough open space to move around. You might need to clear chairs in advance.

The scheme works best in an environment where the children are accustomed to more structured learning.

Recently, I took my scheme into a playgroup. The children were fairly rowdy and initially I found it quite hard to get their attention. I mentioned this, and one of the playgroup leaders said, 'Well, of course they associate this room with playing and running around." It was large and this was the reason it

had been chosen. Size of room, then, is not the only criterion to take into account when thinking where best to teach.

Equipment

First of all, you need a basic kit of instruments for yourself and the children. For the children, these are non-pitched percussion instruments. Suggestions are:

- a triangle (thread a loop of ribbon or string through the top to suspend it by)
- a couple of tambourines (one of them roughly 23cm in diameter)
- three or four maracas
- about three jingle sticks (bells on a short handle)
- about three sets of bells curved around a straight handle (so the whole instrument is shaped like a half moon)
- about five pairs of castanets
- three or four pairs of finger cymbals (like 'normal' cymbals but tiny) (join each pair on a piece of string about 16 cm long to keep them together and make them more manageable for the children)
- three or four egg shakers
- five pairs of tapping sticks (rhythm sticks)
- a drum.

If you can play it, a recorder for yourself would be useful. You might also want a glockenspiel. You could get a wood block too, on which you can beat rhythms (with a wooden stick) for the children to move to.

You can buy these instruments at most music shops, and they are not very expensive, and are very easy to use. You could make simple musical shakers from yoghurt or fromage frais pots filled with lentils, rice, sand, or buttons, then taped together. Tapping sticks can be made from dowling; cut lengths about 1.25 cm in diameter and 15 cm in length, then sandpaper the ends.

You can set out the instruments on a table before the session starts. If you store them in a large plastic crate with handles, or the open type of tool tray with a handle, it makes them portable and also easy for the children to access.

Other equipment you will need is a music stand, and a cassette player or CD player. A piano is not essential, but useful if you can play, or if you know somebody who could come along and play for you. You also need props such as soft toys.

Music Resources

As for the repertoire of music you will use, three songs have been written by the author specially for **The Triangle Club**, and they are contained in Appendix 1. They can be photocopied for your use.

In the Bibliography and Discography, music books, recordings and supporting material have been suggested. You will need to purchase some of these.

Teaching Resources

Appendices 2 to 5 also contain photocopiable material to support you in teaching the scheme.

Starting a Session

As the children arrive, remind them to keep their shoes on, so that they do not slip when running during some of the activities. In order that we are all the same size, begin each session sitting on the floor with the children, in a circle.

Structure and Length of a Session

It is best to follow the same explorative path each week. Thus the children will know what to expect and to anticipate the next activity. Each session lasts forty-five minutes, and there is

a lot of ground to cover in this time, so it is necessary to have a tight structure in which to teach this subject. It would be easy to have a lot of fun but at the end of the course not have achieved very much. It is preferable to offer the children short bursts of activities, which over a period of time become coherent with weekly repetition.

It has already been mentioned that each session consists of eight activities, and these are described in Chapter 3. It is suggested that you keep the scheme intact and use each activity every week. That way you can be assured the children are learning about all aspects of music. But it is also easy to develop each activity, if and when it becomes appropriate. So in Chapter 4, eight extension activities are outlined, one for each of the eight basic activities. To give you a feel for how the author has used the material in practice, sample sessions are illustrated in Chapter 5.

Some tips on timing the session: Plan each session carefully in advance, and keep an eye on the time to make sure you cover each of the activities in the three quarters of an hour.

Managing the Group

Poor concentration can be a problem for some children of this age, and whilst not wishing to pander to it, it is best to change the activities fairly frequently to keep the enthusiasm alive. It is to this end that each session has been carefully designed as a series of eight different activities; and moreover activities which vary between those in which the children are seated, those in which they carry out actions, and those in which they move around. You may need to be quite flexible and ready to move on rapidly to the next activity if concentration is waning.

Another tip: When you first start teaching the scheme, outline your session plan on a large index card or small pad so you can refer to it easily and do not lose track. Then if there are disruptions, you can still move on fluidly to the next activity.

With your knowledge and experience of pre-school

children, you will appreciate that children have diverse learning styles, and this is worth bearing in mind. So even if you have the occasional child who is apparently not listening or engaging, they may, in fact, be absorbing plenty. Rest assured that all this material is entirely suitable for this age group.

Maintaining the interest helps to keep control of the class. By its very nature, music interests and involves children, so you are off to a good start!

The Activities

Introducing the children to the idea of making music in the way we might make a cake, using four basic ingredients

(Start seated on the floor in a circle)

Firstly, ask the children what ingredients are needed to make a cake, what you have to do with these ingredients, and what you get at the end. Ask them about making a musical cake. What ingredients are necessary?

Probably they will not know. You may get some children shouting out "instruments," "guitars" (that is a favourite) and "noise," amongst other good suggestions. But most will still be offering you sugar because you are, after all, talking about a cake! Each week one or two keywords will sink in, and you will soon be encouraged as the children are able to answer you correctly.

Eventually, you will hope for:

a. **High & Low --- -Pitch**
b. **Fast & Slow ---- Tempo**
c. **Loud & Soft ---- Dynamics**
d. **Long & Short -- Rhythm**

The fact that the first two sets of terms rhyme (high and low, fast and slow) helps the children remember them. Do not use the words pitch, tempo, dynamics and rhythm.

To give some meaning to these terms, certain activities are useful here:

- **Pitch** - Jump up as high as you can with your arms in the air, whilst shouting "**high!**" Crouch down low for "**low.**"

Children like to use their voices and this will encourage them to experiment with **high** and **low** registers. It is easy for them to make a **low** sound when they are crouching. The movements are to help them remember the terms. You will say, "We need to have **high** sounds and **low** sounds in our musical cake," and then carry out the appropriate actions with the children.

- **Tempo** - Run **fast**. Walk **slowly**.
  Say, "We need to have **fast** sounds and **slow** sounds in our musical cake," and then do the suggested actions with the children.

- **Dynamics** – Speaking and moving **loud**ly and **soft**ly.
  You will say, "We need some **loud** and **soft** sounds in our musical cake," and suggest ways of making these sounds with our voices and with our bodies.
  Say something in a very **loud** voice. I usually take in a soft toy. I have a Bob the Builder doll that speaks. I ask the children to wake him up by calling his name loudly. ("Wake up, Bob the Builder!") They love doing this. Then we make **loud** movements with our feet, stomping round the room. I then say that Bob the Builder needs to go to sleep, and that we have to move very **soft**ly and sit back in a tiny circle again, where I say we have to whisper his name. You can use the word **soft** even though I appreciate that the opposite of soft is hard and this can confuse initially. But children are quick to learn.

- **Rhythm** – Take **long** steps, like a giant. Take **short** steps, like a pixie.
  Say to the children, "We need to have **long** sounds and **short** sounds in our musical cake," and then carry out the appropriate actions with the children.

The children really enjoy doing these activities. They never tire of waking Bob up! Nor of jumping up

and down, and running round the room at break-neck speed. And the words sink in along with the help of the accompanying actions. It encourages all children to join in. They begin to realise they have control over the sounds their voices can make, and the speed at which their bodies can move.

You need to keep repeating: **high** and **low, fast** and **slow, loud** and **soft, long** and **short**.

Involve the children as much as possible in the making of the cake. Explain that a cake made at home with butter and sugar and eggs is one that we eat, but that when we have made our musical cake we cannot eat it, but we can make music with it.

Activity Two

Activity using voice and basic rhythmic accompaniment (hands clapping)

(Seated on the floor in a circle)

This activity is an ice-breaker whose purpose is to introduce the children to you and to one another in a musical way. Sing 'Who's that Sitting on the Floor?' the music for which is in Appendix 1. Use accompanying actions in 'Who's that Sitting on the Floor?', clapping at the appropriate places in the song. Try to encourage actions only during that part of the song where they are suggested.

You will find that the children will copy what you do. If you get it right, then so will they. Use big gestures to clap your hands. When the song is well known, you can replace clapping with 'tapping' on the floor with your fingertips, then with 'knocking' on the floor with your knuckles. Again, use big gestures. You can also give out instruments to pick up and play instead of clapping.

Encourage all the children to carry out the actions while they sing. At first, you will be singing solo! This is fine. As long as you are confident, the children will eventually join in, some as early as the first session, but others a little later. Some children take a long time, not realising they have such a thing as a singing voice. Doing two things at once is also difficult for young children, but eventually they will do as you do.

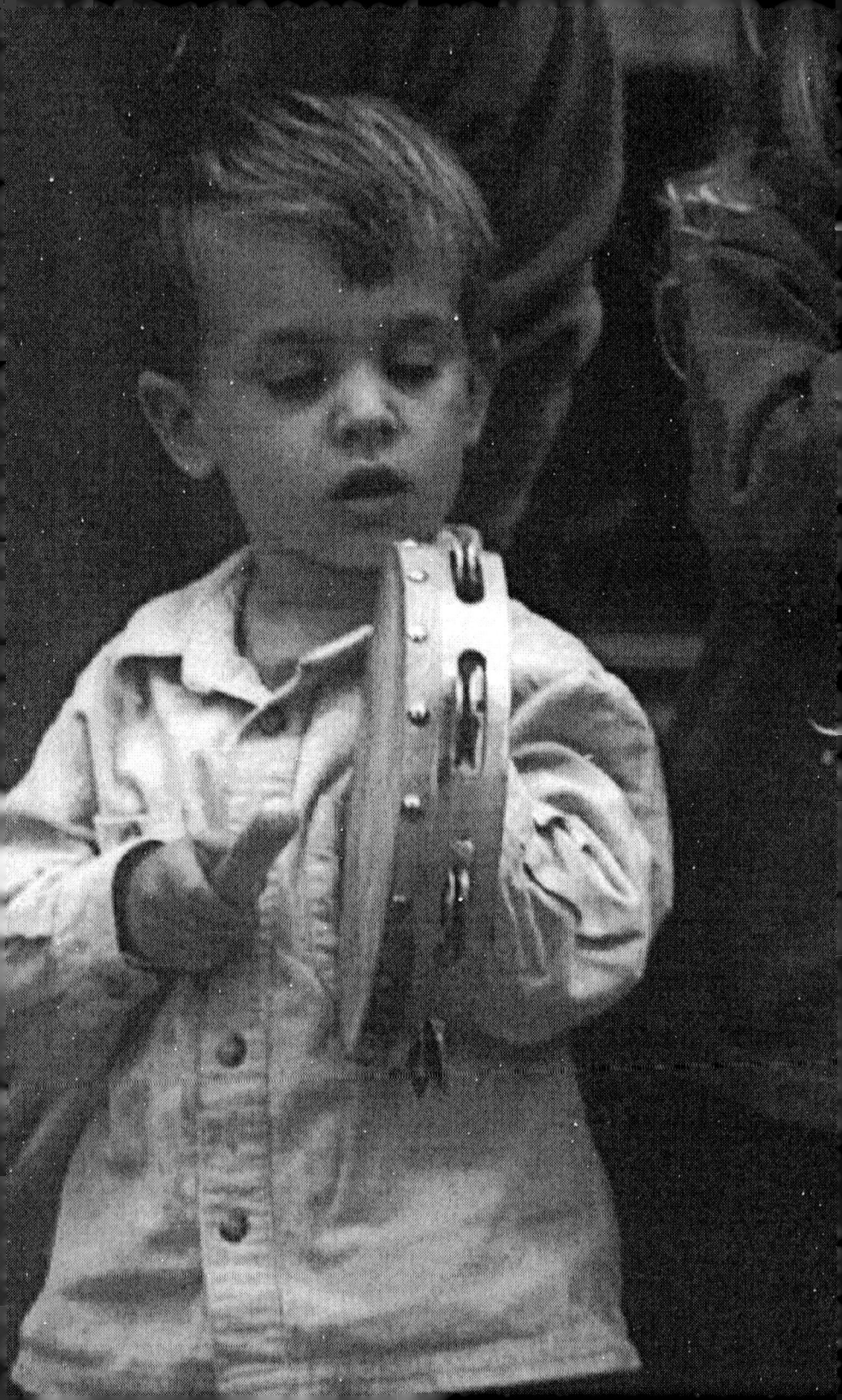

Activity Three

Clapping the syllables in children's names

(Seated on the floor in a circle)

To begin with, it is a good idea to get the children to say their name as they clap it. This helps to reinforce the idea of one syllable, one sound. Examples are one clap to represent Josh, Jack, Jade, Fred, etc.; two claps to represent Chloe, Sophie, Joseph, etc.. You can also clap the names of any toys you might like to have sitting in the group. I bring Noddy and Pooh along in the early stages. You will find that even if a child does not like clapping his name, he will want to clap the toy's name. You will know your children, which ones are shy, and these might be given the toy for support.

After a number of sessions, possibly after half term, I encourage the children to bring in a sheet of paper with leaves or lolly sticks stuck to it. The number of leaves or lolly sticks represents the number of syllables in their names. I show them examples I have made (for Pooh, Noddy and Philippa), so that they can understand what I want them to do. These are included in Appendix 2 as photocopiables for you to use. Some of the children's pictures are included in this chapter.

This work could be done in an art session. It is possible to assess the children's learning throug their pictures.

This is the children's 'music'. Put it on a stand and show that it can be clapped, played on a drum, or tapped on a tambourine. Make it obvious that you are playing on the drum what you are seeing on the 'music' on the music stand. Perhaps someone could point to the 'music' as each child plays it. This enables the children to make a connection with what they see and what sound they produce rhythmically.

Introducing pitch differences is not quite so easy. See Extension Activity Five for an exercise that can be introduced to the children later on in the course.

Introducing the sight-sound connection early is invaluable, and it is so easy to do with rhythm. The children love to be congratulated on reading music and playing what they see to produce this wonderful sound. The important thing is the response of the children to what they see.

Pooh

Noddy

Activity Four

Listening and looking

Have the instruments out on a low table for the children to look at. Let the children touch them, and play them with your supervision, and explore the different sounds they make. Talk about the different voices each instrument has. Experiment with the different ways you can make sounds on these **percussion** instruments. Keep using that word.

Some are **hit** to produce sound, some are **shaken**. Name them appropriately '**hitters**' and '**shakers**'. Explore other ways of making sounds on them. One of the most important things is to show the children how to make the sound stop!

Ask the children what they think that sound could be describing. For example, I say, 'These bells remind me of Christmas, they sound like sleigh bells on reindeer;" "This shaker makes me think of a snake sliding through the grass on his belly."

Set the children some 'work' to do at home; for instance, during the Autumn Term, ask them to listen to autumn sounds (such as wind and rain) when they are lying in bed. Such listening activities will encourage them to discover the world of sound.

Activity Five

Music and movement

The children move around the room while you play an instrument. Initially, use just one instrument so children recognise one instrument, one sound. Over the next few weeks, however, you can introduce more.

Link a particular movement to a particular sound. For example, a loud, booming drum beat can be used to represent a giant lifting large boots and stomping them down again, or walking through deep snow, slowly lifting each foot. Children need to be encouraged to develop slow movements. A triangle could represent hopping. Think of icicles drip, drip, dripping, thus linking sound to an idea. Shake a tambourine for fast falling leaves. There are plenty of ideas here to link into seasons, or animals, or stories you may be reading. This is a good activity to help develop co-operation!

Again, getting the children to stop can be difficult, but extremely important, especially if you want to safeguard your sanity! I usually hit the drum very loudly once and they soon learn this means stop. Congratulate the children on being statues when there is no sound.

Activity Six

Forming a band

You can give the instruments out in a number of ways:

- You can show them to the children and ask them to tell you what each is called. The child that gets it right gets the instrument.

- You can ask the children whether the instrument is a 'shaker' or a 'hitter'. Again, give that instrument to the child who gives the correct answer.

- You can have the children turn their backs to you. This is a very good listening game. You have probably noticed how children listen with their eyes! We are interested in developing the ears and this is a good activity for that. You play an instrument and the child that can come out to the table and play the same one back to you can have the instrument. Make them play it to the others too, asking them if he or she has chosen correctly. It is important to be as inclusive as possible all the time to keep all the children interested and learning.

However you choose to give out the instruments, when each child has one, tell them how important they are, being members of **The (use your playgroup or school name here) Musical Band**.

Then say that you are important too, because you are **The Conductor**. Ask the children what one of these is and what function he or she has. Tell them that a conductor tells the band when to start playing and when to stop, but that he/she is clever because she/he doesn't have to speak. And they are clever too, because they know what to do simply by watching.

Show them that hand signs are enough:

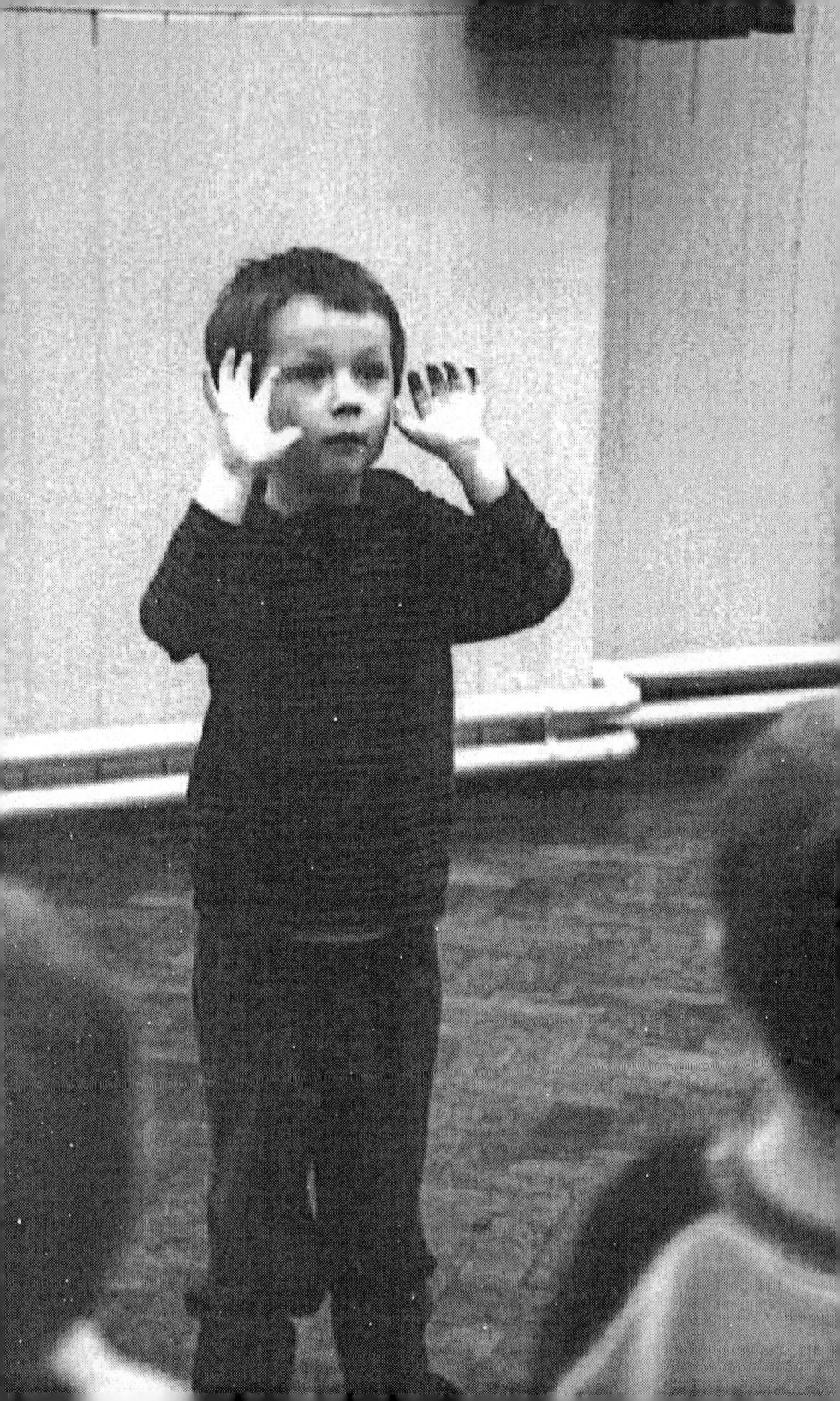

- **Stop**

  With hands stretched out in front of you, palms facing the children, tell them this one means stop.

- **Start**

  Turning your palms to face you, tell them that this one means that they are to start playing.

Of course, watching so they know when to stop and start is the hard bit, because the children will be looking at one another, or at their instrument, or anywhere but at you! However, it will come with practice.

One week, someone will be able to tell you, "You are the doctor!" This is fine. Conductor is a big word for young children, as is percussion, but do not be afraid to use these words.

At first, use big gestures, and use only the stopping and starting gestures. Ask each child to come out and be a conductor. Some will want to as early as the first week. You will often find that children are more able, or perhaps keener, to take notice of their peers than of you. Make sure to join in the band yourself, because you will look at the conductor and start and stop appropriately, and this will encourage the children to do so.

You will soon notice that some children really love to listen to the sound the band is making and are not so keen to use the stopping gesture. Other children love the control and stop and start the band frequently, not listening at all to the sound. We can learn a lot about a child from this game! The important thing here is to get the children to watch the conductor and do what he tells them with his hands.

Eventually, you may want to introduce loud and soft playing:

- **Soft**

  To encourage soft playing, place your fingers on your lips. Keep telling the children that this does not mean stop.

- **Loud**

  To signify playing loudly, stretch your arms out in front of you, then bring your hands towards you repeatedly, with palms facing you (as if beckoning).

Gradations of 'loudness' and 'softness' in music are know as dynamics. When children try to vary the dynamics, they will often vary the speed at which they play. For example, when playing softly, children will often play slowly, and when given the direction to play loudly, they automatically speed up their playing. Not only children do this! Be sure to point out to them what is happening, and get them to listen to it. Then encourage them to try again playing loudly and softly, but this time without varying the speed.

Watch your children and try to encourage all sorts of combinations of playing. One possibility is to split the group into two, and ask them to do different things alongside each other (for example, half of them play loudly while the other half play softly).

Activity Seven

Singing songs

(Seated on the floor in a circle)

Towards the end of each session, to put the children in the mood for listening during the final activity, sing a few simple songs with them. I use the same four songs for about five or six weeks. These can mark a special event (for example, Easter or Christmas, or a non-Christian event, introducing children to songs from other cultures). Or they can reflect the weather, or introduce or connect to other areas of learning. I use a lot of counting songs. Songs can provide a sing-song for the children and can help to forge them into a happy group.

Watching children discover their singing voices is a wonderful thing.

Suggested songs to start with, all of which are easy for children to learn and sing, are 'Rain on the Green Grass', 'Topsy Toe', and 'An apple' (all from **Diddly, Diddly, Dumpty**), and 'One Rag Doll' (from **Counting Songs**). (Details of these song books are given in the Bibliography.) All the songs in Jane Hart's compilation are suitable too.

This activity seems to be the one that worries adults most. Yet it is also the activity that most adults do with their children. If you know that you really cannot sing in tune, or if you are very anxious about singing, then do sing along with a tape. The Early Learning Centre stock a variety of song tapes for children. It is important that children hear singing that is in tune, but it is also important for them to hear those they have direct contact with singing, so do join in. Singing must not be seen as something difficult, a source of embarrassment, or something that others do.

When you are teaching the children a new song, you could play the tune to them first on the recorder or the piano (or get a helper to do this).

Activity Eight

Listening to some recorded music

(Seated on the floor)

This is my favourite activity. It gives you the opportunity to introduce children to music and composers that they may not have access to, and also to musical instruments.

If you need an introduction for yourself first of all, have a look at the books listed in the Bibliography under 'Other Books to Use'.

Introduce the children to musical instruments and their various sounds with a brilliant recording called **The Musical Life of Gustav Mole**. (Details are given in the list of 'Recorded Music' in the Bibliography.) This has an accompanying book, which can help you. Using the book alongside the tape can help to focus the children on the activity in hand. Play just a couple of pages, depending on time. But remember this is an important activity, so try not to run out of time or enthusiasm. The story is really appealing to young children. There is a real delight in following the little mole growing up, surrounded by his musical family and friends.

I sometimes use cards or pictures to show the different instruments. I recommend the card game **Musical Families: Learn About Instruments**, which is listed in the Bibliography.

Suggestions of music to move on to after **Gustav Mole** are given in the next chapter.

Concluding Comments

This brings us to the end of the scheme and the session. As you use **The Triangle Club Music Scheme**, you will discover how it establishes a solid foundation of musical knowledge. It also links into your curriculum for the under fives. You can see how much work there is inherent in the scheme, and will appreciate that as it stands, it needs no development. It is a scheme ready to be used.

However, it can be developed, if and when you choose, to suit your needs as pre-school teachers. The following chapter outlines eight extension activities, one for each of the scheme's eight basic activities.

4

The Extension Activities

Extension Activity One

Activity One involves thinking about music as a whole, and can stay basically the same throughout - though you need not always use Bob the Builder! I have a soft toy which plays the violin when a button in his shoe is pressed. This delights the children because an arm moves to push the bow over the violin. They love to wake him up!

You can develop the activity by counting the children in ('One, two, three.'). Make this part of the activity. Or choose a *child* to count in before you jump, crouch, run, walk, shout, whisper, and take long or short steps. This way you are teaching the children to anticipate something, and then all start together. Remind them that they need to count in loudly.

When they are walking slowly, repeat that 'slow' does not have to be 'soft'.

An extension of this could involve playing taped music and asking the children what they heard. For example, was the music loud or soft, fast or slow, did the tune go up or down? Simple questions favouring one-word answers. What you are doing is getting the children to think about how music is made up.

The Swan from Saint-Saëns is an example of slow, expressive music. *The Wild Asses*, also from *Carnival of the Animals* is an example of very fast music. I always draw children's attention to the part in *Peter and the Wolf* where Peter is letting the rope down to catch the wolf by the tail, and at this point in the music the instruments play a descending scale to illustrate this.

Extension Activity Two

Activity Two also rarely varies, but you can introduce other ideas. For example, when the activity is really familiar, sing the boys' names loudly and the girls' names softly. You can also change the tempo (speed). That way the children are kept on their toes, really having to follow your direction. When the song is well known, give out instruments to pick up and play instead of clapping.

Make sure you frequently ask for the children's opinion. 'Shall we sing the boys' names loudly ...?', etc. Anything to stop an activity from becoming dull, whilst retaining the original idea of the exercise. Use one hand, then both hands to tap, then you could use feet. The important thing is to keep each task simple, so that all can eventually join in and sing. If you have a big group, you may not want to sing every child's name, so suggest something like singing the names of all the children with red socks on.

You can appreciate that the children are learning about lots of things as well as music by participating in this scheme. When to join in fully and when to wait your turn are invaluable exercises in learning to be a musician.

I use 'Who's that Sitting on the Floor?' at every session during the whole of the Autumn Term. During the second term, I introduce the idea of happy and sad music by using an ice-breaker song that involves the sound of **major** (happy) and **minor** (sad). I wrote my song 'Are You Sad?' specially for this purpose, and it is given in Appendix 1, ready for you to photocopy.

I explain to the children that the song uses the word 'glad' to mean 'happy', because 'glad' rhymes with 'sad'. I also explain that the song is all in the minor, and sounds sad, until the very last line. Then, on the words 'No, I am glad!', the music alters to the major, which sounds happy.

In the Summer Term, I teach the children 'The Triangle Club Song', which is also in Appendix 1. I leave it until then because it is slightly more complicated. The children love

joining in with all the activities (clapping, turning around, jumping, crouching). Use your conducting skills and conduct the children! Get them to alternate between loud and soft; they have to look at you to find out which.

You could, if you wish, make your own choice of other appropriate introduction songs which involve children's names.

Extension Activity Three

The theme of clapping the syllables in a child's name can be extended in various ways. Names can be played on different percussion instruments. This is a good opportunity to teach the children how to hold, and then control, the instruments. Some instruments are easier to control than others. Start with the drum. Pass it around the circle. Another variation is to get a child to play another child's name.

Children love to play their favourite chocolate (be content with two syllables for choc'late) or television programme or character. Get them to clap or play these. For example, two claps for Rolos, three claps for Milky Way. I also ask the children to clap or play what they had for breakfast or lunch.

This can be quite interesting! The children have to be clear in their minds and really think about what they are clapping or playing. As in Activity Three, to begin with, get them to say the word as they clap it, in order to reinforce the idea of one syllable, one sound. Eventually, you may like to guess while the child is only playing and not saying.

You can develop this further by clapping longer words and phrases, or nursery rhymes. 'Humpty Dumpty' is a good one because of its strong rhythmic sounds. Have a reserve of three or four nursery rhymes that you can choose from to clap or play on a drum to the children for them to guess. I also use 'Twinkle, twinkle, little star', 'Baa baa black sheep' and 'Jack and Jill', especially the first two, which are very similar.

Eventually, they will be able to pick one nursery rhyme out from amongst two or three others that you clap or play to them. As with all the activities, you model the activity for the children to copy. You could then give the drum to a child to play whilst you and the others in the group guess. You could clap a line of the nursery rhyme, the children clap the next and so on.

A great game to play is to have corners in the room for the children to walk to when they hear different rhymes played on a drum. This game, like most of the activities in the Triangle

Club Music Scheme develops the ear and the memory as well as developing a rhythmic awareness.

At this point, you may want to introduce the sight-sound connection as identified in Activity Three. This can be developed to incorporate producing 'music' which identifies certain foods; for example, 'fish fingers and chips' using five lolly sticks. A lolly stick picture of this has been included in Appendix 2 for you to photocopy and show the children. Varying the size of the sticks could introduce the children to reading long or short sounds. Play this appropriately.

This is the children's first step in reading a simple musical notation. Put the 'music' on a stand and make a point of reading from the music, showing them that you are able to produce the correct rhythm because you are looking at the 'music'.

Extension Activity Four

Activity Four can be used as a springboard for a variety of different activities.

You will most likely have only non-pitched percussion instruments. You will have been talking about these. You will have explained that some have to be shaken and some hit to produce sound, whilst some (such as the tambourine) can be both hit and shaken. Explain, though, that not all instruments are played in this way. Introduce other instruments with pictures; the section of the Bibliography entitled 'Other Books to Use' mentions a couple of books you could use here. Better still, introduce instruments with the real thing if possible. Maybe someone you know plays an instrument that they would be happy to show to the children during one of the sessions. This can be a real treat.

In the Spring Term, when you are listening to **Peter and the Wolf** (see Extension Activity Eight), draw the children's attention to how clever Prokofiev is to choose the various instruments to represent each character. For example, he uses the high fluttery notes of the flute for the bird, and the rather melancholy sound of the oboe for the duck. We all know the terrible end that awaits the duck! Encourage them to use their imaginations.

Using pictures in an instrument sorting activity can be fun. This works well in a small group. You could talk about the different families into which instruments are grouped. (These are shown in Appendix 6.) It is at this point that I might give out a worksheet called 'Spot the Odd One Out', to consolidate work done in the session. You can photocopy this sheet from Appendix 3.

This activity can be quite difficult and may require a lot of support. You will need to know how instruments are grouped into 'blowers' (either woodwind or brass), or stringed instruments (bowed or plucked), or percussion (both pitched and non-pitched), and which instruments belong to each family. The card game **Musical Families: Learn About**

Instruments, which I have mentioned already, works well here to reinforce this information. (It is listed in the Bibliography.)

You could use this time to show instruments from different cultures. This would be especially relevant if you could also play them an example of music from that country later on in Activity Eight.

Extension Activity Five

This is fairly easy to develop, but bear in mind that the basic idea of getting the children used to starting and stopping is the object of the exercise. They will also be developing an ear for the different sounds which instruments are able to produce. Any movement you wish to use can be represented by a musical sound. Be clear and firm about this, because children love to run around, and need to be encouraged to respond to different sounds. Sometimes you can see from their movement that they have not identified the musical sound correctly. For example, the maracas (perhaps representing a slithery snake) could sound to some children like the little egg shakers (perhaps representing gliding through the snow). Remind them to listen very carefully, so that they respond to the sound with the appropriate movement.

Try to encourage the children to listen rather than keep looking to see what you are playing. Stopping can be a big problem for some children. As in many of these games, 'you are out!" may be required! You may like to have a helper.

Choose a child to play some of the instruments with you once you have developed the game sufficiently. Some instruments are harder to play for little hands.

Talking about high and low sounds (pitch) could also occur here. For this activity, you will need to be able either to play a pitched instrument (for example, a recorder or glockenspiel), or to use your voice. I think the spring is a good time to introduce this, and if you have had the children since the autumn, they are ready for a stab at understanding the concept of pitch.

Get them to crouch down low, representing a tiny seed in the earth. Move by step only. Get them to grow as the music you play gets higher, then shrink back down as the music gets lower. The children like to do this.

After a while, get them to grow at different speeds according to the tempo (speed) of the music you play.

I introduce the 'sol-fa ladder' here. This is easy for you to

learn from Appendix 5, which you may photocopy. Basically, you sing step by step up or down a 'ladder' of notes, singing each one to its own syllable ('doh', 'ray', 'me', etc.). As you do this, you make a different hand signal to indicate each note.

Alongside the 'graphic notation' of the leaves, the 'sol-fa ladder' gives children their first introduction to making a connection between sight and sound.

Using the hand signs, I ask the children to make their voices climb up the ladder. I ask them to sing these signs as they go upstairs to their beds. And they do, I have been told by bemused parents! Eventually, a child will be able to make a number of the signs, and sing these too as you sign them. Make the hand signs very clear, using large gestures for the children to follow. Then a child might like to come out with you and do the signs himself for his peers to follow. This is quite a difficult task, but one that can be learned.

Getting the children to realise that their voices can go up and down is a valuable thing. You need not always go by step, once you feel confident and the children are ready. For example, you could skip or jump, using the hand signs to signify this by moving from 'doh' to 'me', etc.. This is perhaps the most difficult activity, and need not be attempted. It is there for you to use when and if it becomes appropriate, not for you to worry about.

As you feel more comfortable using the signs and your voice you could sing 'Hello children, how are you today?" Using *soh me soh me, soh soh me me soh?* For them to answer 'Hello Ting, we feel okay today." using *soh me soh, me soh soh me me doh.*

There are plenty of songs which use some or all of the rising and falling scale to help you interest the children in using the full range of their voices. One I use is in the song book entitled **Counting Songs** (which is listed in the Bibliography), and is called 'Seven Little Steps'. I would use this in Activity Seven in conjunction with working on pitch in the present activity.

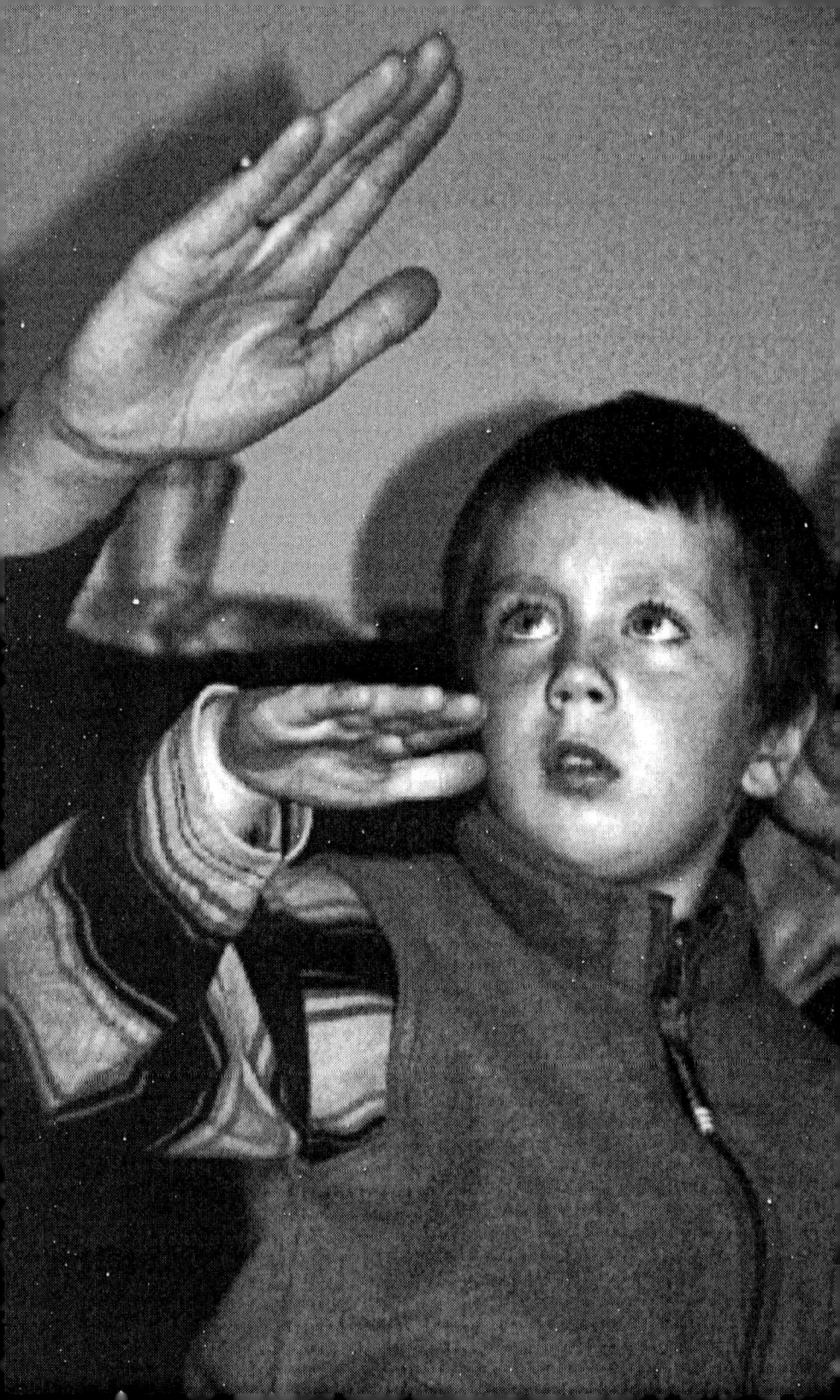

Extension Activity Six

Activity Six is a wonderful activity for young children, who are usually all keen to use the instruments. Before you start, make clear the gesture for stopping, and explain the reason for them all to look at the conductor. Do not make this activity too complicated. Children love just to play, and this is really the only chance they get, so it is a good time for them to be a bit free with sound. You can teach them gestures for playing 'loud' and 'soft' (described with Activity Six). Playing loudly seems to go quite naturally with playing fast, and playing softly is often equated with playing slowly. You will need to encourage other kinds of playing. You could split the group in two and have a cacophony of sound.

You could have the 'hitters' in one group and the 'shakers' in another. Children need to be constantly encouraged to listen to the sound they are producing and to think how they are making it happen.

They enjoy conducting, and some children develop quite sophisticated gestures to get their band to follow them. When you are confident and the children are happy, you could 'play' a particular idea; for instance, a giant walking (loud sounds) which then becomes a mouse walking (quiet sounds, which can be fast, as a mouse moves quickly). You may want to introduce the idea of solo playing by pointing to a single child, or just a couple of children. Use your imagination and let the children use theirs. But keep it very simple. The beauty of this activity is that nothing is wrong. Some things might be more successful than others. Talk about them and suggest improvements or alternative instruments.

I often use the piano in this activity, too, rather than a conductor, to get the musical band to move round the room. The children soon learn to respond to starting and stopping to the sound of music. If you have someone who can play the piano, then choose one or two pieces of music from which to play. You can vary the dynamics, and choose music that may be marching music or skipping music.

Try to encourage the children to move appropriately.

Extension Activity Seven

This is simply up to you. It can be varied to suit your lesson plans. You can use counting songs, songs about the four seasons, songs celebrating special occasions. Try to involve simple movements in some of your songs. 'Heads, shoulders, knees and toes' is very popular and in its entirety is a good warm up. I like to teach three or four simple songs and then stay with them for about five weeks. There are lots of good books which link into every aspect of a child's life experience s and learning.

I like to extend this activity by linking it to a children's story. I found a wonderful book, **Three Tapping Teddies**, which is in the Bibliography. It contains musical stories for the very young, and I have used, amongst others, the Little Red Riding Hood, Goldilocks, and Cinderella stories from it with great success.

This can take a good deal of time, and I suggest that you do not attempt them until you have really covered the basics and feel that you are confident and the children are ready to tackle something slightly more ambitious. These musical stories really do challenge the children and are excellent activities in themselves to aid the learning process.

When you do decide to use one of these, it is a nice idea to give a performance of it. The Cinderella story works particularly well here, with you telling the story to cue in the children with their different voices and instruments. In the **Three Tapping Teddies** version of the story, everything is in threes (for example, 'ma-gic wand'), and is a real feat for the children to count in threes, and say things in threes, and play in threes.

There are several songs I use which demonstrate changes of speed (tempo). Two that the children love come from the Jane Hart book. One clearly shows music speeding up (p 94), the other, music slowing down (p 98). Children need to 'feel' music and their body, like their voice is their very own special instrument.

Extension Activity Eight

I especially enjoy this activity, where you can introduce the children to real music, and also introduce them to composers. It can be helpful to show pictures, thus drawing the children's attention to something in particular. But do make this a *listening* activity. Learning to listen takes time and practice. Begin here and now. Try not to talk over the music.

In term two, I move on from **The Musical Life of Gustav Mole** to **Peter and the Wolf**, and then in term three, to **Carnival of the Animals**.

Peter and the Wolf is good to use after **Gustav Mole**, as it concentrates on a more limited number of instruments, and in this way can be more thorough. Before the story proper begins, there is an introduction telling you which instrument is linked to each of the characters. This will help you as well as the children. I recommend two publications to use with the recording. One is a beautifully illustrated book which you can show alongside listening to the musical tale. In this book, **Peter and the Wolf** is retold and illustrated by Ian Beck. The second is an arrangement of **Peter and the Wolf** for easy piano by Carol Barratt, which contains the text and lovely pictures. Details of both are given in the section of the Bibliography and Discography entitled 'Recorded Music and Supporting Material'.

Talk about the composer, Sergei Prokofiev. Show a picture of him. And tell the children one or two things about him. Children love to be shown pictures of composers and told little stories about the times in which they lived.

After a while, get the children to draw pictures of the characters, linking each to the appropriate instrument. For example, the wolf is represented by the horns, the duck by the oboe. The children can do so much creative work around this wonderful music.

My next choice, which will take you to the end of the year's course, is **Carnival of the Animals**. Once more, you are introduced to the instrumentation before the story itself

starts. For **Carnival of the Animals** I recommend using with the recording an arrangement for piano (by Hans-Günter Heumann) plus story and pictures, details of which are again given in the Bibliography.

Again, talk about the composer, in this case Camille Saint-Saëns. And once more, ask the children to do some drawings, linking a instrument to an animal. Some children's pictures for **Peter and the Wolf** and **Carnival of the Animals** are reproduced in Examples 3 and 4 in the next chapter.

I am constantly amazed at what appeals to young children. They can remember little details and you can see how a musical awareness and memory is beginning to develop in a general as well as in a more specific way. I give out pictures of the composers and anything that I know will interest them and enable them to listen more intently. For example, one of the animals in **Carnival of the Animals** is the tortoise. Saint-Saëns writes cleverly for this animal, using Offenbach's 'Can-Can', but slowing the tempo to convey the idea of these slow animals dancing. I show a picture at this point of tortoises, in frilly knickers, kicking up their legs doing a very slow version of this dance. This drawing is included as Appendix 4, and is photocopiable.

Little things like this capture children's imagination, and aid concentration, and memory. The children also never tire of counting how many times the lion roars as he leads the procession.

This is a brilliant way to introduce children to instruments and their particular sound. You can use any music that you think is valuable. Music from other cultures always interests children. At one pre school I visited recently, one of the leaders played some Chinese music, and delighted the children by also bringing in a very large, very colourful dragon! This was a delightful excursion into another culture.

Concluding Comments

I hope you are beginning to see how easily each activity can be used to complement and reinforce other areas of learning. Once you are confident about using the scheme in its simplest form, you may feel you want to adapt it. But I want to impress on you that your children are getting all they need to develop their musical ability from the scheme used in its original layout.

My scheme is for you to use within the context of your individual playgroup or school. As you are developing the scheme, you will see that you may be spending more time on one activity at the expense of another. But most of the activities are interlinked. We are, after all, involved in making music. The separation of my scheme into eight activities is to make it easy to understand, to teach and ultimately to learn from. You may decide to use only one or two of the activities for a few sessions, and develop these to accompany other things that are taking place within your school, such as a concert for a special occasion. (For instance, see Example 2 in the next chapter.) After this, however, I do advise you to go back to doing the scheme in its simplest form, especially at the beginning of each term.

I have deliberately not been specific about when to introduce slightly more difficult activities because this will vary from school to school. You may find that after the first five or six weeks, you are ready to work on Little Red Riding Hood as part of extending Activity Seven. You may even feel you could give a little performance in front of parents at the end of each term, in which you sing a few songs alongside this longer story/song. Performing at an early age can be a wonderful experience.

I am sure that many of you will have been giving your children music activities along these lines already. Part of my intention here has been to show you the value of what you are doing, and also to take the activities on to the next stage, where you do not just feel you are giving a child a drum to

bang about on once a week. Once you appreciate the significance of banging on a drum and singing a few songs, you will be better able to teach the children in your care.

The next chapter contains some more ideas for ways of extending the scheme.

5

Practical Experiences –
Sample Session Plans

Laid out for you now are four examples of my session plans for some lessons I have recently taught using **The Triangle Club Music Scheme**. You will see how some of the activities receive more prominence as a particular event comes upon us. You will also see examples of some of the children's work, all of which has been done at home with help from parents, and then proudly brought back to show me.

I always appraise each session, making a note of what worked well, what needs to be developed now, and what still needs reinforcing in its simplest form. I assess each child's development as we go along in a notebook. I don't have to give reports but I do give feedback to parents about their child's progress. Some parents do use these music sessions, but more especially the Music is Fun Music Scheme, which follows on from the Triangle Club, as an introduction to more formal instrumental lessons, and will then ask specific questions about suitability of child to instrument.

My session plans are set out very simply. They can of course be set out more formally, showing aims and objectives, and the outcomes, and teaching methods, with details of resources. Written details of evaluation and assessment methods are always useful too for 'next step' proposals. Session plans laid out in this way can be very helpful as it enables you to be very focused.

Feedback, however, from playgroup leaders suggests that a more informal plan allows for more flexibility. Teaching in pre school is not so heavily prescriptive as the National Curriculum is for year 1 onwards. But it is still very necessary to ask questions about the learning which has taken place, so it is valuable to reflect on each session, asking yourself quite searching questions. If you are clear about the learning aim then the learning outcome should match it. For your interest, I

append my session appraisal to the first of the sample session plans.

EXAMPLE 1: Autumn Term, Session Five

Activity One

The children are gradually learning the ingredients for making a musical cake and are confidently using the words **high & low, fast & slow, loud & soft, long & short**, and moving confidently too.

They like pretending there is a large mixing bowl in the middle of the circle, and that they are using a huge wooden spoon to stir all the ingredients up together. I shall encourage a child to count us in now. The children are beginning to appreciate the need for a clean start, which means us all starting at the same time, and are learning to anticipate beginnings.

Activity Two

No change to this activity, except to begin to ask the children how we should sing the song. This encourages them to really think about how they can manipulate the sound they make, both the tempo (speed) and the dynamics (loud and soft). Maybe we could split the class into girls and boys, and alter the speed for one group. I shall ask them for their opinion.

Activity Three

Today I am going to take in the leaf diagrams I have done. They show a very simple kind of graphic notation. My sheet shows Noddy and Pooh. (This is in Appendix 2.)

I want the children to use leaves to denote their own names. This will enable them to make that early connection between what they see and what they hear. I shall set this

task for them for homework, so will talk to parents about it at the end of the session. If there is time, I shall encourage every child to have a go at playing from the leaf diagram. I shall use the drum to demonstrate and offer it to them to play on. Must take in a music stand for the ' music' .

Activity Four

Today I shall take in a scrapbook of pictures of instruments. I shall ask the children to look through catalogues and, with Mum's or Dad's help, cut out pictures of instruments to bring in to show the group next week. Today I shall talk for a short time about how certain instruments are played. We have already heard various instruments and imitated playing them whilst listening to our recording of **Gustav Mole**. I shall explain that the percussion instruments on our table are unable to produce a variety of pitches as other instruments do. I shall continue to play my recorder to illustrate a pitched instrument.

Activity Five

Must ensure that the children are able to stop. I may have to be strict here and have an 'out corner' for all those who will not stop to be statues. I shall enlist a helper and introduce some more sounds to link to a movement, for them to play. As winter approaches, I shall suggest a triangle for icicles dripping. The triangle is quite difficult for small hands to manipulate and this is a good opportunity to ensure each child has a turn at developing their technique when playing one.

Activity Six

I shall keep the activity at its simplest, as time will be running out, and more and more of the children like to have a turn at conducting.

Activity Seven

This will be the last time we will sing the songs I have taught the children so far. I shall say that I just want to hear them, so I shall not be singing very loudly. Most of them have learnt the words and are happy to sing now. The four songs I have taught them proved to be well liked. (I have used those suggested in Chapter 3.)

Activity Eight

I may not leave myself enough time to do justice to the listening activity today, but will ensure I have some time to put the tape on and encourage good listening. The children are enjoying this very much. We will continue to work through **Gustav Mole** until the end of term. I have been drawing their attention to Frog being a fine fellow playing the 'cello. We all imitate him playing the 'cello and various other characters playing other instruments.

Session Appraisal

After this session, I decide to introduce the Little Red Riding Hood story/song the following week, in Activity Seven, and work on it for a number of weeks until the end of term. The children now realise that they have different voices, gruff and sweet, loud and soft, as well as their singing voices. I decide to begin teaching Christmas songs alongside this.

I am anxious that the children begin to feel the pulse (beat), which is inherent in all music, as different to tempo and rhythm. Teaching pulse is very important and I rather feel that I need to address this with the children. My intention will be to instill an inner metronome—the ability to feel an ongoing beat or pulse and then introduce rhythms over the top. I will do this by getting them to copy me clapping a steady beat of 4 claps, making clap **1** the loudest to reinforce the pulse. For example: **1,2,3,4 / 1,2,3,4**. Over this steady clapping, I will sing Humpty

Dumpty. I will introduce songs which will help the children to 'feel' a strong pulse/beat, and encourage them to clap the pulse/beat whilst we sing the words. The words, happily, follow the rhythm in songs, so this is easy to understand.

EXAMPLE 2: Autumn Term, Session Nine

My term is ten weeks long, and at our last session (next week) we are putting on a Christmas concert. Because this is coming up, concert practice will be taking over a lot of our time. But that is as it should be.

So at this session, I shall merge the activities so that rehearsals incorporate all eight activities. They will all still be there for us to use as separate activities when school resumes in January. The children and I shall then be pleased to resume the scheme in its entirety.

I have been working towards the approaching concert. The songs have been learnt and just need to be rehearsed with a performance in mind. I shall keep telling the children how exciting performing is, how their Mums and Dads and Grandmas and Grandpas will be coming to hear *them* sing and not *me!* I shall assure them that I shall be in front of them mouthing the words and conducting, so that any instrumentalists will know when to come in.

Little Red Riding Hood proved a success with the children, who are now able to recall their singing voices, their speaking voices, their grumpy voices, etc..

I chose three songs for this half term - 'Ding - Dong!' and 'Robin', from **Diddly, Diddly, Dumpty**, and the traditional carol 'Oh Christmas Tree', and one to get them moving, 'Here We Come a Carolling'. This is one they can clap to, dance to, skip to, etc. It is from a book of Do it Yourself Nativities, by Vera Gray. The bells work well on 'Ding – Dong!', and castanets and sticks on the 'Robin' song, the instruments joining with the singing on 'hopping on the carpet, picking up the crumbs'. Triangles are lovely for 'Oh Christmas Tree', but are difficult to control, so need plenty of practice today, so they do not interfere with the pulse.

Even when I merge the activities, I always make sure I have time for the listening activity (Activity Eight). I want to finish **Gustav Mole** so I can begin **Peter and the Wolf** next term.

EXAMPLE 3: Spring Term, Session Three

Activity One

> The children are happy to keep making the musical cake to begin each session. They are aware that not all instruments can 'do' high and low, which has enabled me to develop the idea of pitch in Activity Five. Also, beginning with Activity One in its entirety settles the children and focuses their minds. They are now all able to tell me that we come here to make music. Also, I have new children coming in throughout the year, so it ensures that no child misses out. The others are always overjoyed to tell them what is what!

Activity Two

> The new song, 'Are You Sad?', is awakening their ears to the sound of major and minor (happy and sad). I shall use it interchangeably with 'Who's That Sitting on the Floor?' (Both the songs are contained in Appendix 1)

Activity Three

> We are able to play a really large repertoire of rhythms now, both from memory and using simple notation. Most of the children are able to say immediately what I am clapping, and then join in with the clapping. Today I shall ask some children to come out and play rhythms on the drum for the others to guess.
> It is important to make each task as interactive as possible.

Activity Four

The card game **Musical Families** is a real favourite and the children are beginning to be able to sort the instruments into families easily. Today, I shall try the game, showing them the instruments only, without the animal pictures. I shall ask the children questions about last week, when they were shown a guitar and a violin and were able to play these and hear them being played. It will be interesting to find out just how much the children remember about the way the instruments were played, the sound each produced, the size, etc. This will enable me to assess the benefit of last weeks session.

Activity Five

The children are beginning to use the hand signs of the 'sol-fa ladder' quite fluently up to 'soh'. I shall continue to play the recorder, getting them to grow from seeds to plants, and will develop this idea by varying the speed at which the plant grows, and then returns to being a seed again.

I shall also introduce them to the idea of painting the wall! On the piano, I shall play the same tune three times at different pitches. The children have to paint high up the wall, on the middle of the wall, and low down the wall, depending on what they hear.

Activity Six

Today I shall ask the children to think about ways they could 'play' 'giants' or 'cats' or 'mice' using the percussion instruments. I shall draw their attention to instruments that might be better at doing the 'job'. I shall also tell them why (for instance, big instruments can make bigger or louder sounds, whilst little instruments play softly). By this stage, they should be making intelligent choices, showing you that you are

successfully developing their ability to discriminate. We can then work on this over the next few weeks.

Or I might get them to work in pairs, with an instrument for each pair. One child will play the instrument; the other has to move appropriately. After a while, I shall ask them to come back into the group to show us their work.

Activity Seven

Today, I shall introduce them to the Goldilocks song/story, using **Three Tapping Teddies.** (This is listed in the Bibliography under 'Song Books'.) The children are enjoying the new songs and are learning both the words and the tunes. It is good to see how their memories are improving. They are enjoying the song 'Seven Little Steps', using the hand signs to help make our voices go up and down.

Activity Eight
Peter and the Wolf is brilliant! The children love it. Today I shall ask them to do some homework for me: to draw a picture linking a character to the correct instrument. We will talk about this for a while.

EXAMPLE 4: Summer Term, Session Six

Activity One

Because rehearsing all that we are doing for the summer concert is taking up more and more of our time, this activity has to be shortened to simply raising our hands for 'high' and bringing them down for 'low', running our fingers over the floor 'fast' and then moving them 'slow', shouting 'loud' and whispering 'soft', and then taking a few 'long' steps and a few 'short' steps.

Activity Two

The new song, 'The Triangle Club Song' (in Appendix 1) is good. The children love clapping, and are beginning to clap rhythmically and turn round in time to begin the next phrase. I use this song interchangeably with the other two in Appendix 1.

Activities Three, Four, Five, Six and Seven

I shall link these together now for the last few weeks to enable time for relaxed rehearsal.

The songs need to be known really well for the children to sing them confidently in front of an audience. 'How Do You Feel....?' and 'The Spider Song' (both in **Songs from Play School**, which is listed in the Bibliography). The children are having fun with tempo/speed changes and we have been working on this over the past few weeks. I like

to have songs which encourage movement so that children learn to 'feel' music, and the two songs mentioned earlier from the Jane Hart book are good examples of tempo changes and have delighted the children, who like to change the speed at which their bodies move. They especially like to ride their horses at varying speeds, and then to drop down exhausted at the end of "I see the Pony Galloping". We are also to include a performance of the Cinderella song/story. This has been a great success with the children, who are happy to play the instruments in the

appropriate places, use their voices at different levels of volume, and do a variety of actions now. All this is very gratifying and demonstrates the progress that has been made over the past few months.

There is a great deal of activity going on here. A good mix of singing, movement, playing of instruments, with all children participating. In a group it is vital to be able to differentiate, and you will know which children are capable of playing and singing at the same time, and which of them needs encouraging to do so.

Activity Eight

I have a long way to go to finish **The Carnival of the Animals**, so must allow time for this activity. I shall ask the children to do some drawings again, linking an instrument to an animal.

Concluding Comments

I hope this has been in some way helpful in showing, without being too dictatorial, how I have used the basic activities to develop ideas I have had for teaching music to the children in my care. I have tried to show you ways in which you can use the scheme that encourage musical development. But I have also been at pains to show you how you can use the scheme in ways that reinforce other things that are going on in the curriculum; and more importantly, that once you have covered the basic idea of **The Triangle Club Music Scheme**, it can become yours for you to use and develop as and when you are happy to do so.

Afterword

Dr Montessori, according to Bernarr Rainbow, had 'stumbled upon an important factor in musical education when she stated that a valuable way of heightening aural sensitivity consisted 'not in producing, but in eliminating as far as possible, all sound from the environment'."[6] I never feel guilt when I force silence on children! After all, before Montessori, musicians such as the composer Robert Schumann had realised the importance of developing the ear. And really listening is a difficult thing to do.

We are always surrounded by noise. A good listening game is to sit in silence and really listen.

To begin with, the children do not hear anything! I tell them what I have heard: the birds singing; the wind through the leaves; a noisy van; a plane perhaps; the radiator; or the sound of the electric light. In this way, music can be said to be all around us, connecting us to many things, both great and small, significant and less significant. When we learn to listen, we can feel this connection.

Music-making must not be kept a secret from adults or from children. If this book has helped to demystify music and the acquiring of musical knowledge, then I feel I have gone some way towards reducing the problems surrounding the teaching of music to young children.

I hope to have shown you how easy it is to do.

I have certainly enjoyed teaching many children over the years and, more recently, developing the scheme to teach it to adults.

In the words of Giles Andreae, a favourite children's author, in his book **Giraffes Can't Dance**, 'We all can dance, when we find music that we love."[7]

Notes

1. M. Montessori, **The Discovery of the Child**, trans. M. J. Costelloe S. J., Clio Press, Oxford, 1988, p. 145.

2. Don G. Campbell, **The Mozart Effect: Tapping the Power of Music to Heal the Body, Strengthen the Mind and Unlock the Creative Spirit**, Hodder and Stoughton, 2002 (ISBN 0340824379). See too Don Campbell and Joseph Pearce, **The Mozart Effect for Children: Awakening Your Child's Mind**, Hodder Mobius, 2002 (ISBN 0340820926).

3. M. Montessori, **The Discovery of the Child**, trans. M. J. Costelloe S. J., Clio Press, Oxford, 1988, p. 144.

4. Ibid., p. 58.

5. Ibid., p. 59.

6. Bernarr Rainbow, **Music in Educational Thought and Practice**, Boethius Press, Aberystwyth, Wales, 1989, p. 283.

7. Giles Andreae, **Giraffes Can't Dance**, Orchard Books, London, 1999, p. 28.

Appendices

Appendix 1

[PHOTOCOPIABLE]

Specially Written Songs

BY TING RANDLE
© Ting Randle

Note

Music used in this section can be transposed to fit in with the children's vocal range. It is written here in the key of C to avoid confusing sharps and flats.

Who's That Sitting on the Floor?

Ting Randle

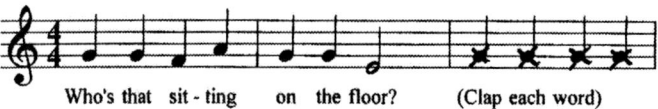

Who's that sit - ting   on   the floor?   (Clap each word)

Ma - ry   is   her   name.

(Clap)   Are you read - y   to

sing with us?   (Clap)

Mu - sic   is   our   game!   Yes!
                                   (and clap)

Notes shown as ✗ show rhythms for clapping.

Are You Sad?

Ting Randle

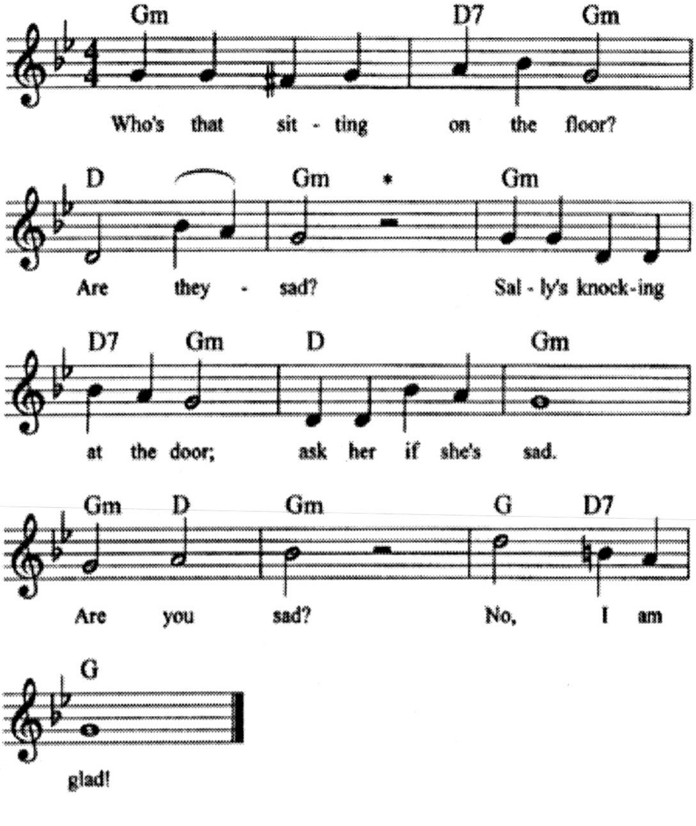

Who's that sit - ting on the floor?
Are they - sad? Sal - ly's knock-ing
at the door; ask her if she's sad.
Are you sad? No, I am
glad!

* Child tells you her name

The Triangle Club Song

Ting Randle

Let's all clap our hands! (Clap)

Let's all turn a - round! (Turn around)

Let's all jump up high, then sit down on the ground.

What is your name? Ste - ven is his name.

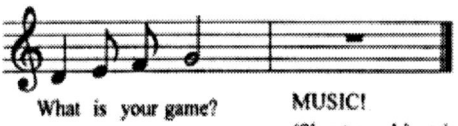

What is your game? MUSIC!
(Shout or whisper)

* Let child tell you his name.

Alternate between loud (f) and soft (p). The children have
to look at you to find out which. Use your conducting skills!

Appendix 2

[PHOTOCOPIABLE]

Leaf and Lolly Stick Pictures

The purpose of these images is to help children make the connection between what they see and what they play. This works well with rhythmic phrases such as Fish Fingers Chips and Peas, which would have six lollies of different sizes, each representing a syllable. Two different lollies are required to represent the long and the short in music, with the half-eaten lollies representing shorter words or sounds.

Pooh

Noddy

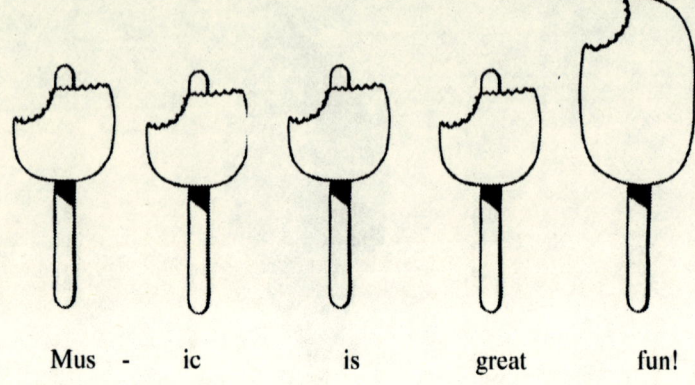

Mus - ic   is   great   fun!

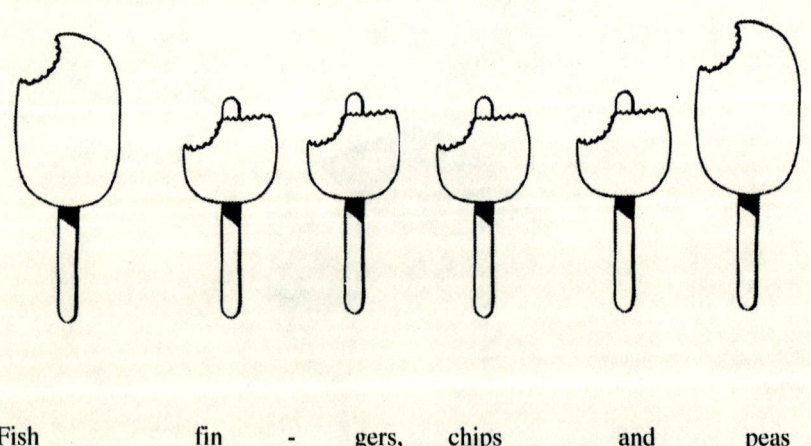

Fish   fin - gers,   chips   and   peas

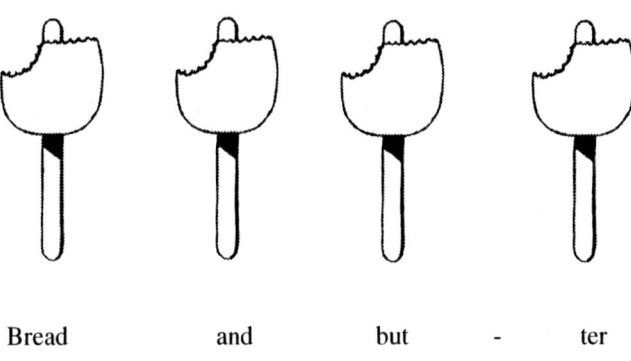

| Bread | and | but | - | ter |

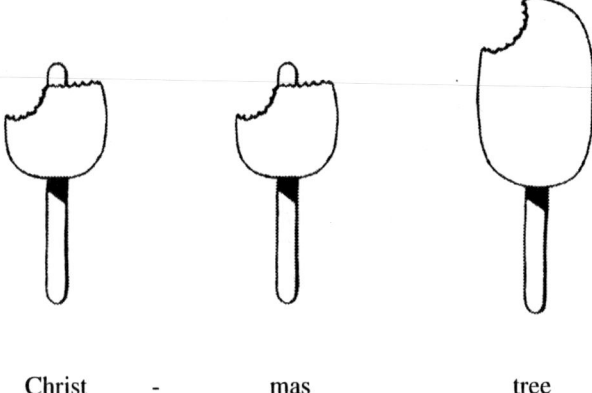

| Christ | - | mas | tree |

Overleaf are two lolly graphics that can be photocopied and used to represent names, words and phrases to help expand the children's understanding of, and familiarity with this idea.

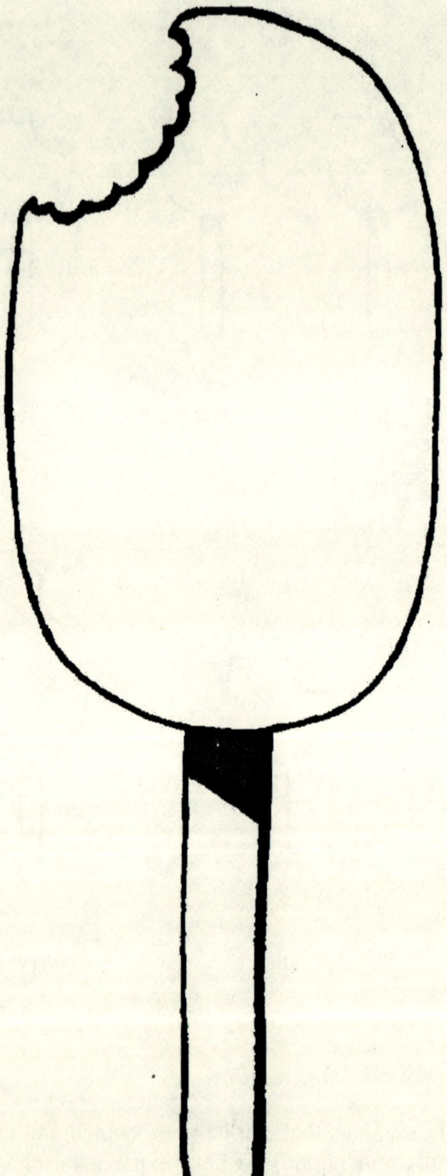

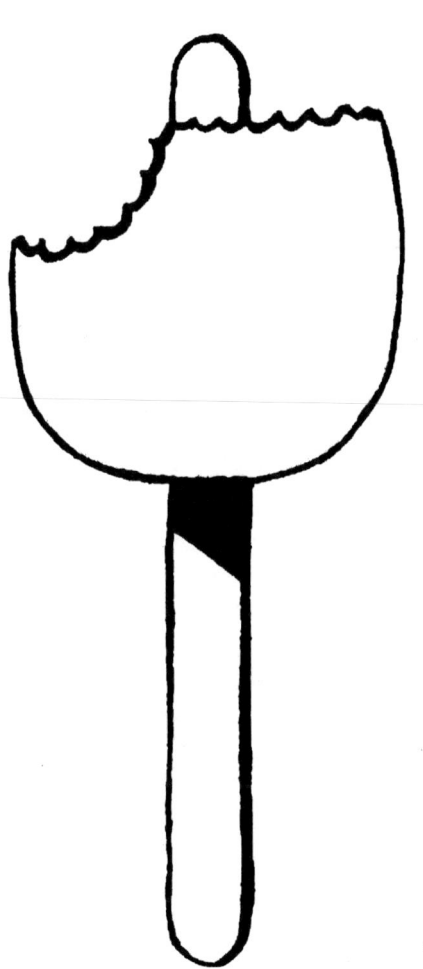

Appendix 3

[PHOTOCOPIABLE]

'Spot the Odd One Out' Worksheet

'cello

tuba

trombone

singer

triangle

maraccas

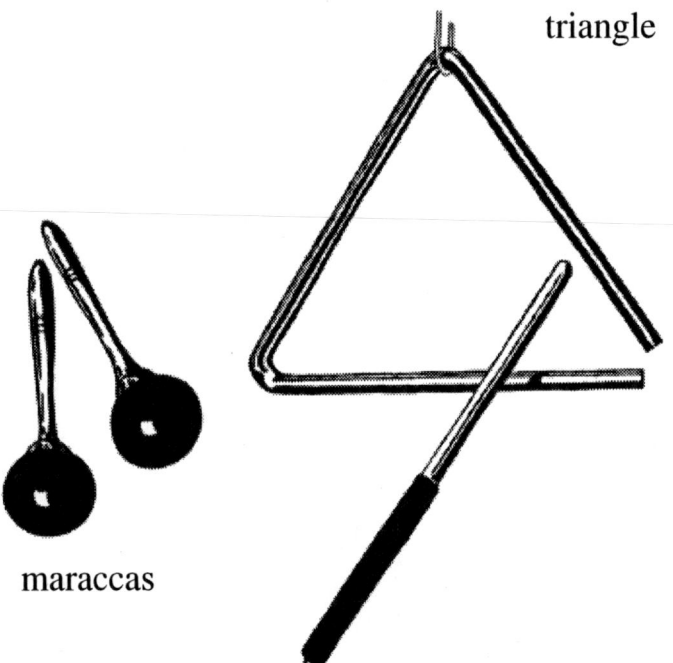

drum

clarinet

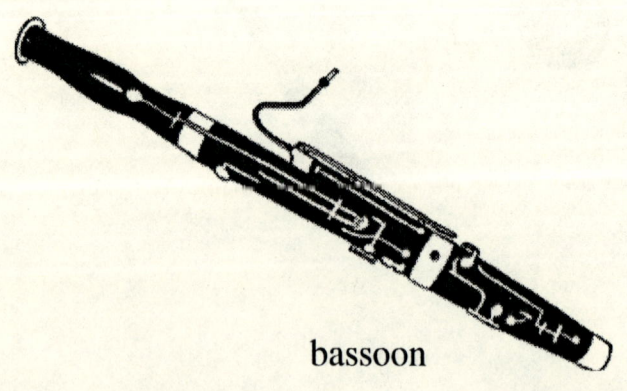

bassoon

trumpet

violin

'cello

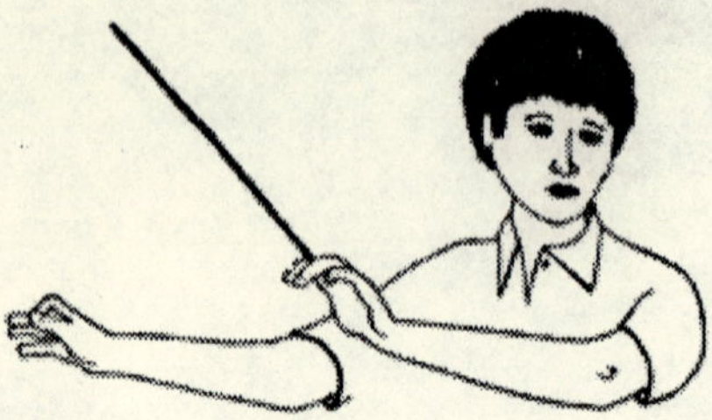

conductor

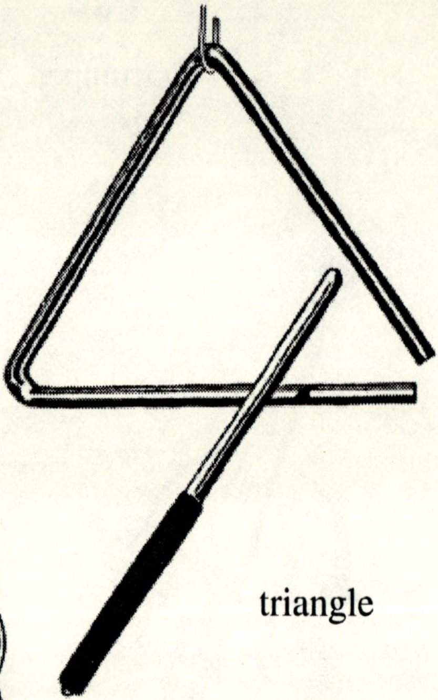

triangle

drum

flute

harp

clarinet

bassoon

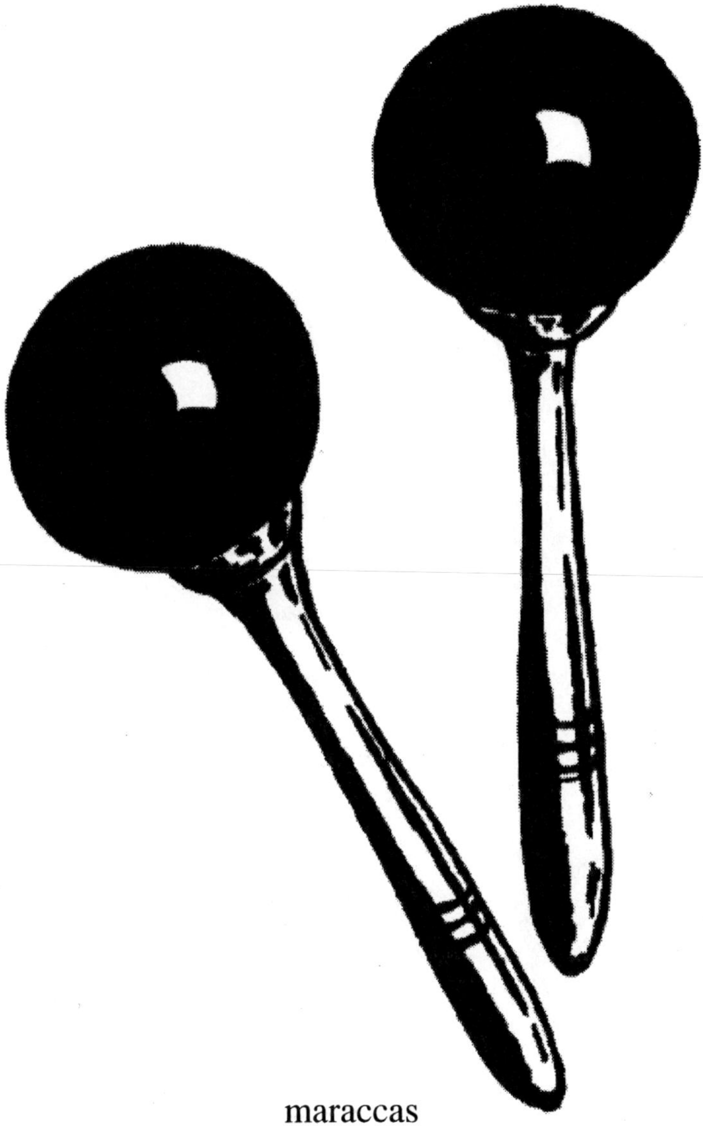

maraccas

'cello

clarinet

drum

flute

harp

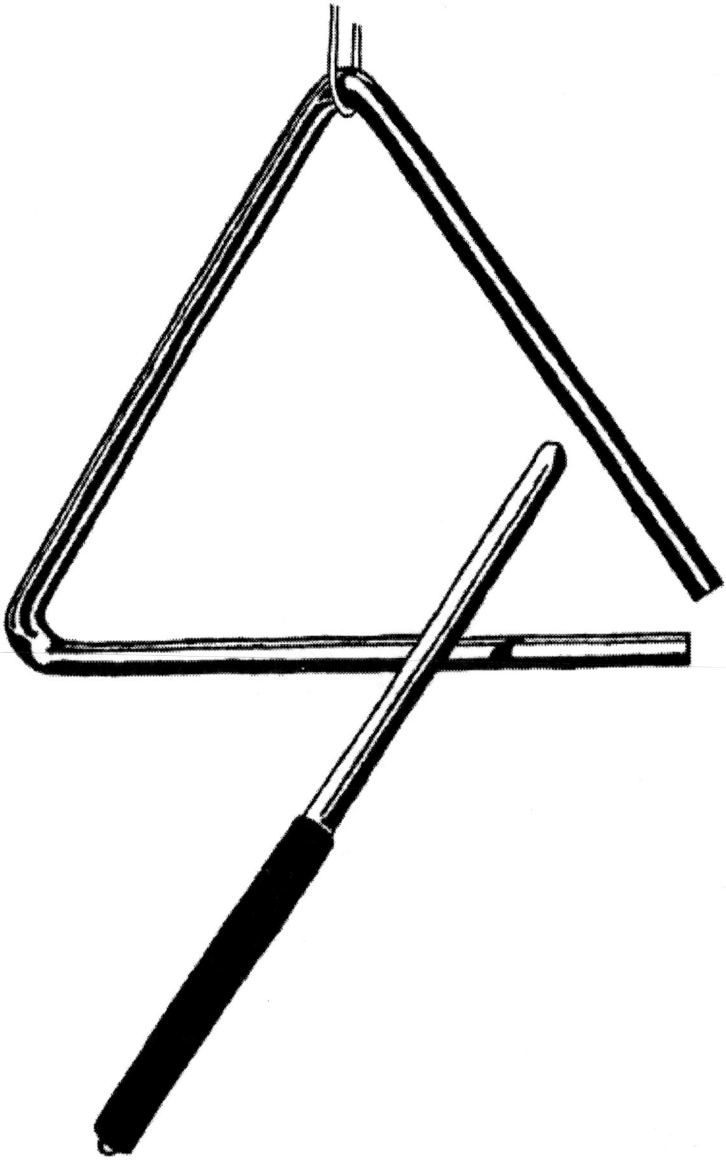

triangle

trombone

tuba

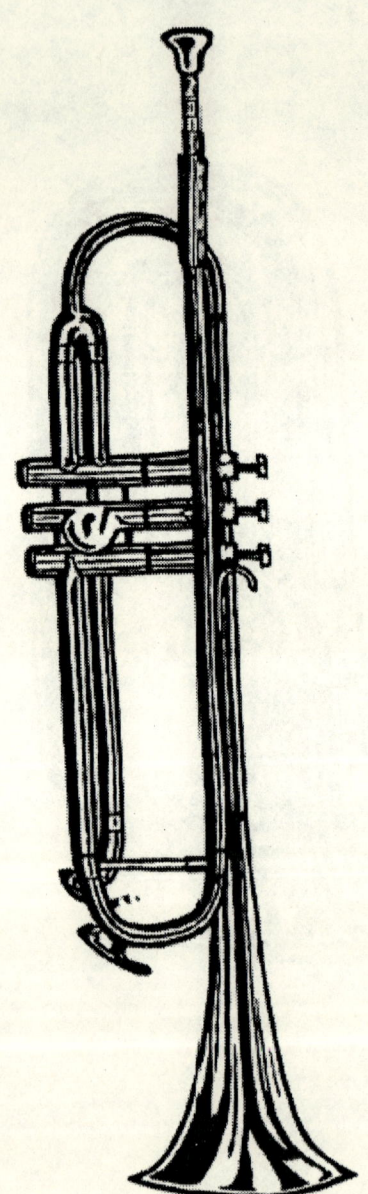

trumpet

violin

Appendix 4
Carnival of the Animals

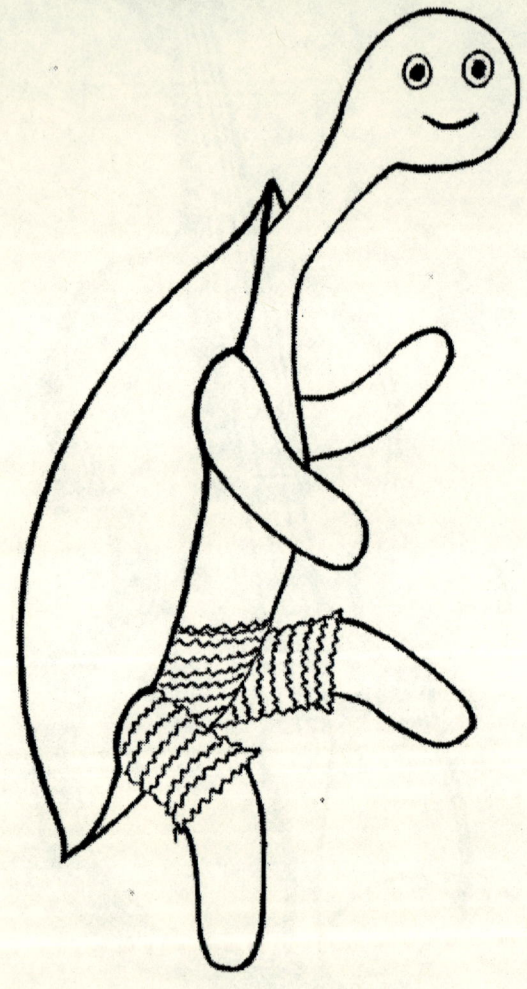

© Pete Randle

Wolf—represented by the horn

Flute

Bird—represented by the flute

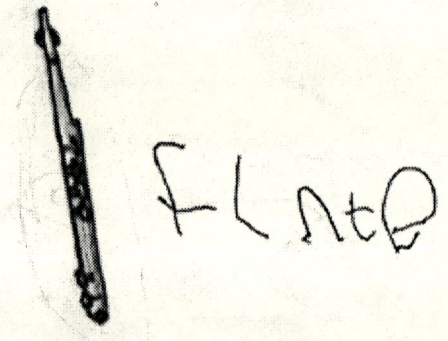

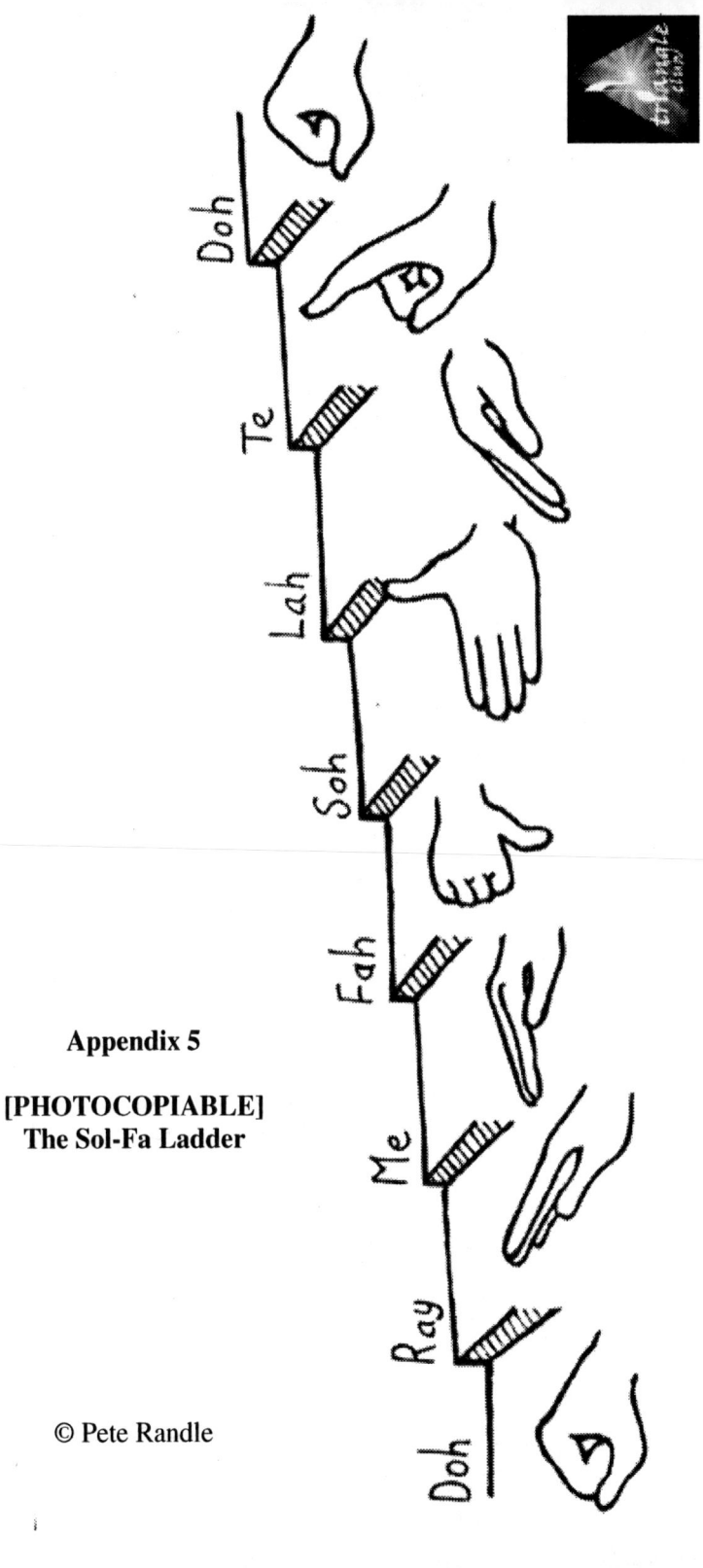

Appendix 5

[PHOTOCOPIABLE]
The Sol-Fa Ladder

© Pete Randle

Appendix 6

Instrument Families

<u>Note</u>: If you need an introduction to instruments for yourself, see the books listed in the section of the Bibliography entitled 'Other Books to Use'.

Stringed Instruments

<u>Bowed</u>

Violin
Viola
' Cello
Double Bass

<u>Plucked</u>

Guitar
Banjo
Harp

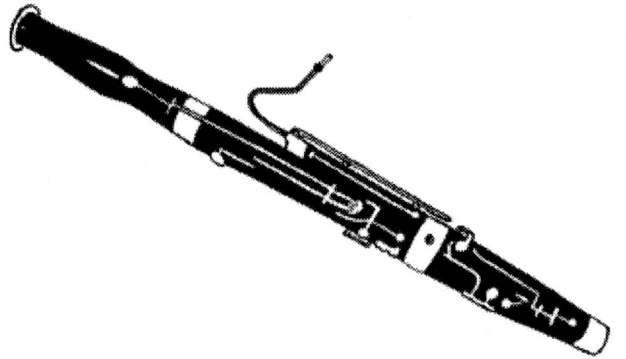

Woodwind

Flute
Oboe
Clarinet
Bassoon

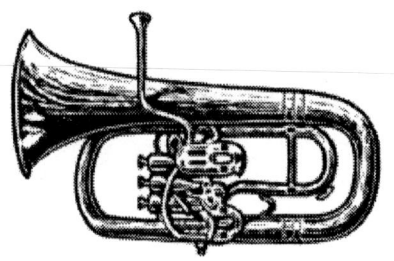

Brass

Trumpet
Horn
Trombone
Tuba
Cornet

Percussion

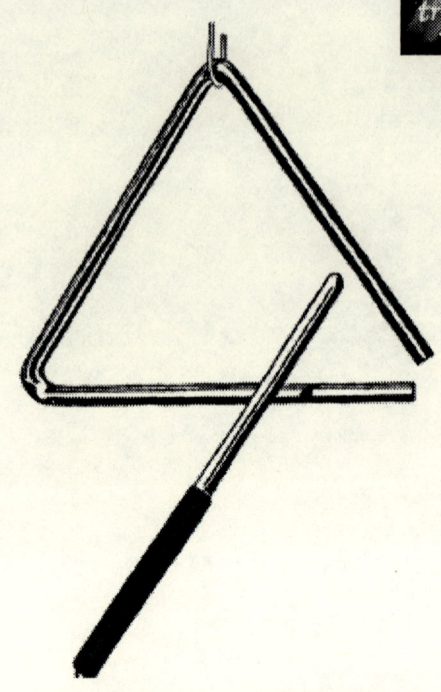

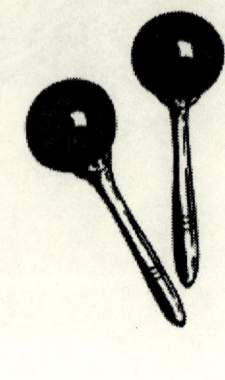

Non-Pitched
Drum
Tambourine
Triangle
Maraccas
Bells
Castanets
Cymbals
Egg Shakers

Pitched

Glockenspiel
Xylophone
Piano

Appendix 7

Some Musical Terms Used in this Book

Chord – More than one note, usually three, sounded together.

Crotchet – The note which is written as ♩. The longest note currently used is the *semibreve* (𝅝), which is also known as the whole note, and this functions as the basic unit of length or duration of a sound. It is divided into two minims (𝅗𝅥), or half notes, four crotchets (♩), or quarter notes, eight quavers (♪), or eighth notes, and so on. So a crotchet can be thought of as a one-beat note (where a semibreve lasts for four beats, a minim for two beats, and a quaver for half a beat). There is a clear explanation at the beginning of the song book **Counting Songs**, which is listed in the Bibliography.

Degree of the scale – The notes of a scale can be described as the degrees of the scale. The first note of an ascending scale is called the key-note or first degree; the second note is the second degree; the third note, the third degree; etc..

Dynamics – Gradations of loudness and softness in music.

Graphic Notation – Music written in pictures or using pictorial symbols. The children's leaf music is an example of this.

Key – If a piece is based on the notes of, for example, the scale of C major, that piece of music is described as being in the key of C major. Each note in a particular key is classified as having a specific relation to a note known as the key-note, which is the most important. So in the key of C major, the key-note is C, and all other notes have a subordinate role.

Major – This term describes how the music sounds. I link it, as

do many others, to a happy and bright sound. The word itself refers to the key a piece of music is in.

Minor – Again, this term refers to the key of a piece. I would suggest that the music sounds sad.

Non-Pitched Percussion – Percussion instruments which produce sound of indefinite pitch. You cannot alter the pitch of these instruments.

Ostinato – A persistently repeated melody or rhythm. Think of 'obstinate', which is the translation!

Pitch – The 'high'- or 'low'-ness of musical sounds.

Pitched Percussion – Percussion instruments of definite pitch; for example, a glockenspiel, which has a set of tuned metal bars which are hit with two small hammers.

Quaver – See '*Crotchet*' above.

Rhythm – Aspect of music concerned with the duration of musical sounds. Patterns of long and short sounds distributed within a regular pulse ('heartbeat').

Scale – A succession of notes which move upwards or downwards in steps from a starting note. A scale of C major, for example, uses the notes C-D-E-F-G-A-B-C.

Sol-fa ladder – This introduces the tonic sol-fa, which is an English system for notating music by means of syllables. It was introduced in the 1840s by J. S. Curwen (1816-80), and is used for ear training and to train singers in sight-reading. According to tonic sol-fa, the notes of the major scale are named (in ascending order) with the syllables 'doh', 'ray', 'me, 'fah', 'soh', 'lah', 'te ', 'doh'. These were made famous by Julie Andrews in **The Sound of Music** in

the song beginning 'Doe a deer, a female deer'.
    With the sol-fa ladder, you sing step by step up or down a 'ladder' of notes, s inging each one to its own syllable. As you do this, you make a different hand signal to indicate each note. You can easily learn to use the sol-fa ladder from Appendix 5, which is photocopiable.

Tempo – This refers to the speed at which the music is played or sung or moved to.

Timbre – Tone colour; quality of the sound of a particular instrument or voice.

Bibliography and Discography - Suggested Material For Use With Pre-School Children

Song Books

Note: If you have limited funding, **Diddly, Diddly, Dumpty**, **Counting Songs, Singing Games and Rhymes for Early Years** and **Three Tapping Teddies** are the four essential song books.

The Best Song Book Ever compiled by Jane Hart (Victor Gollancz Ltd., London, 1983, ISBN 0575032758).
This book contains everyday favourites with easy to play piano arrangements and guitar chords. Some of the songs have directions for actions and movement.

Boomps-a-daisy chosen by Peggy Blakeley and Sue Williams (A & C Black, London, 1986, ISBN 0713656018).
Forty singable songs with simple piano accompaniment and guitar chords.

Counting Songs by Peter Canwell (Early Learning Centre, London, 1987).
Twenty-two traditional and new counting and number songs, arranged for voice and piano or guitar.

Diddly, Diddly, Dumpty by Lilian McCrea and Kathleen Staton (EMI Music Publishing Ltd., London, 1979).
Action songs for the very young. This is a brilliant book, containing finger plays, face games, action rhymes, and fun songs for all seasons.

Songs from Play School compiled in association with BBC TV, illustrated by Tony Ross (A&C Black, London, 1987,

ISBN 0713656050).
A book which links in to the wider curriculum, with piano accompaniment and guitar chords.

Three Tapping Teddies by Kaye Umansky (A&C Black, London, 2000, ISBN 0713651180).
Musical stories for the very young. Creative, accessible and totally entertaining. Brilliant book, no need to read music. It combines literacy, numeracy and musical development.

Singing Games and Rhymes for Early Years by Lucinda Geoghegan

Do It Yourself Nativity by Vera Gray. Lindsay Music ISBN 0858580223

Song Books for Slightly Older Children

Harlequin by David Gadsby (A&C Black, London, 1981).
Forty-four songs round the seasons. Contained here are songs for all seasons with piano accompaniment, guitar chords and extended curriculum activities. There is even a recipe and directions on how to make a windmill!

Okki - tokki – unga. Action Songs for Children chosen by Beatrice Harrop, Linda Friend and David Gadsby (A & C Black, London, 1976, ISBN 0713616857).
Included are '55 songs for nodding and wagging, for tapping and hopping, for waving and singing and shouting'. There are simple piano accompaniments and chords for guitar.

Tinder-box chosen by Sylvia Barratt and Sheena Hodge (A&C Black, London, 1982, ISBN 0713621702).
Sixty-six songs to make children think or laugh, with piano accompaniment and guitar chords, complete with instrumental parts for all to join in. A good one to introduce ostinato accompaniment.

Other Books to Use

Simple Science. Sound and Music by Barbara Taylor (Kingfisher Books, London, 1990, ISBN 0862725283).
This is a very practical book with lots of things to explore with sound and music.

Sound and Music by Kay Davies and Wendy Oldfield (Wayland Pub. Ltd., Hove, 1991, ISBN 0750202831).
This book shows you how to explore sound and music for yourself.

The Orchestra by Mark Rubin (Oxford University Press, Oxford, 1984, ISBN 019272206).
A lovely book with pictures introducing all the instruments of the orchestra.

Understanding Music by Judy Tatchell (Usborne Publishing Ltd., London, 1990, ISBN 0746003021).
An Usborne Introduction to instruments, composers, reading music, science. This is a good introduction for you to keep you one step ahead!

Educating the Whole Child. An Holistic Approach to Education in Early Years by Sandip Hazareesingh, Kelvin Simms and Patsy Anderson. (Building Blocks Educational 1989 ISBN 0951428802)

Card Game

Card Game. Musical Families. Learn about Instruments invented by M. Twinn, with illustrations by Kathy Meyrick (Child's Play (International) Ltd., Swindon, England and New York, 1989).

Recorded Music and Supporting Material

The Musical Life of Gustav Mole. Book by M. Twinn, illustrated by Kathryn Meyrick, with cassette, narrated by Patrick Macnee (Child's Play International Ltd., printed in Singapore, 2000, ISBN 0859533336)
This is a brilliant introduction to music for very young children.

Peter and the Wolf by Sergei Prokofiev. Various recordings are available. I use the version in which Sir John Gielgud narrates the story, but there are also recordings in which it is narrated by people such as Dame Edna Everage, David Bowie and Patrick Stewart.

Peter and the Wolf retold and illustrated by Ian Beck (Doubleday, London, 1994, ISBN 0385403437).
A beautifully illustrated book to show alongside listening to the musical tale.

Peter and the Wolf. A Musical Tale for Children arranged for easy piano by Carol Barratt (Boosey and Hawkes, London, 2002, ISBN 0851622690)
This contains the text and lovely pictures.

The Carnival of the Animals by C. Saint–Saëns, arranged for piano by Hans-Günter Heumann, story by Loriot, translated by Timothy Moores (Schott Musik International, Mainz, 2000, ISBN 3795755069).
This contains pictures.

CD: Children's Classics—Peter and the Wolf, The Young Person's Guide to the Orchestra, Carnival of the Animals featuring Sir Ralph Richardson, Sean Connery. London Symphony Orchestra conducted by Sir Malcolm Sargent. (Decca Karussell UK Limited, 1993)

About the Author and Acknowledgements

I graduated from Dartington College of Arts in 1992. I was a mature student when I went there, already having had three of my four children. To suggest that I have experimented with my ideas about music education on my children sounds outrageous and a little cruel, but I fear it is true that I have done so! I do not think they have suffered unduly. I moved to Wells, Somerset, in 1999, when my eldest daughter won a scholarship to study the piano at Wells Cathedral School. Both my teenage daughters are currently piano scholars there. My eldest son is a guitarist and my youngest, who is now four, is a keen Triangle Club goer. All my children have been.

I have learnt a lot from them. In fact, all the children I have taught have taught me something.

I taught class music for ten years at Greylands Preparatory School where the headmistress Pauline Adams was very keen to develop an holistic music education for the children in her care. She allowed me a free rein with the music curriculum. This I enjoyed and was really where I developed my ideas for teaching music. I developed **The Triangle Club Music Scheme** whilst working for Alan Morris, Director of Music at Paignton Community College. In fact, the name was his idea. Thank you, Alan. I have refined the original idea over the years and believe that as it stands, it offers an accessible, adventurous and hugely enjoyable way for children and adults to participate in early music making.

Currently I have a busy piano practice. I teach **The Triangle Club Music Scheme and the Music is Fun Club** to children and to playgroup leaders, and teachers in Primary Schools, who want to take over the scheme and teach it to children themselves. I tutor for Wells Adult Learning and Leisure. I have access to lots of music making and teach a range of people of all ages and abilities, the youngest being three years of age and the oldest eighty one. I am class music teacher at Leigh-on-Mendip First School. I believe that music should be for everyone to enjoy and get pleasure from.

I would like to thank Gill Deamer, whose suggestion to offer the Triangle Club Music Scheme here in Wells set the ball rolling for all this activity. I want to thank Will Webster for helpful advice.

I want to thank my publisher, Dave Randle at Bank House Books, for the interest, endless patience and enthusiasm with which he has received my book.

I first met Catherine Hudson at a party. I discovered that she too had been a student at Dartington, where she trained as an actress. She had subsequently lived in London, working for fifteen years in theatre, television and film. In 1983 she won the Best Actress Award at the Arezzo International Theatre Festival in Italy. After marriage, two children and moving to

the West Country, she had decided to extend her passion for the Arts, and retrained, taking the Art Foundation Course at City of Bath College, where she discovered her love of photography. She had since staged several exhibitions.

I thought then how I would like her to do the photographs for this book. A short while later I came across her work at an exhibition and decided to ask her if she would consider taking the photographs. It struck me as important to have a visual explanation of the scheme I had set out, so that the activities could be immediately understood. Where words often fail, pictures reveal an answer. I am grateful to her beyond words.

I also want to thank my children, who have been a constant link for me into the making of music. Their enthusiasm has encouraged me and their delight in the world of music has confirmed for me just how important music and music making is in people's lives. I want to thank Pete, who has supported me throughout the writing of this book and offered me so many suggestions for ways to improve it. His diagrams throw light on the text and I am very grateful for anything which does that.

I would also like to thank Jo Bellchambers, whose constant support has encouraged me to go on with this project when time seemed so short and more pressing things needed to be done. With a family, there are always more pressing things to be done then setting down words on a page!

I want to thank Pam Roberts, who is the Adult Learning and leisure Co-ordinator in Wells. She has supported me with **The Triangle Club Music Scheme** from the outset. Her faith has encouraged me to set down these words on the page. This has often been a nightmare, as I am not a writer. Pam's interest in it has been very valuable to me. I also appreciate very much all the help which Julia Wood has given me with this book.

I would like to thank the schools who have asked me to teach them the scheme. Their response to it and the feedback I have had from them has been enormously encouraging.

I would like to thank all the children who have participated in **The Triangle Club Music Scheme** and have given

drawings that I have taken the liberty to use in this book. They have made the scheme such a joy to teach. Thank you also to the parents who have brought them to me each week.

Last but not least, I would like to thank my parents, who, when I was a young child myself asking for music, gave it to me without question.

Ting Randle

For demonstrations or further information, visit the Triangle Club
Music Scheme website at:
www.ting-randle.co.uk

Printed in the United Kingdom
by Lightning Source UK Ltd.
103570UKS00003B/1